How to ᴗs
the ADI Exams

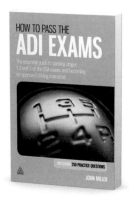

How to Pass the ADI Exams

The essential guide to passing parts 1, 2 and 3 of the DSA exams and becoming an approved driving instructor

John Miller

KoganPage

LONDON PHILADELPHIA NEW DELHI

Publisher's note

Every possible effort has been made to ensure that the information contained in this book is accurate at the time of going to press, and the publishers and author cannot accept responsibility for any errors or omissions, however caused. No responsibility for loss or damage occasioned to any person acting, or refraining from action, as a result of the material in this publication can be accepted by the editor, the publisher or the author.

Crown copyright has been reproduced by permission of the Driving Standards Agency which does not accept any responsibility for the accuracy of the reproduction.

First published in Great Britain in 2012 by Kogan Page Limited

Kogan Page Limited
120 Pentonville Road
London N1 9JN
United Kingdom
www.koganpage.com

© John Miller, 2012

The right of John Miller to be identified as the author of this work has been asserted by him in accordance with the Copyright, Designs and Patents Act 1988.

British Library Cataloguing-in-Publication Data

A CIP record for this book is available from the British Library.

ISBN 978 0 7494 6519 3
E-ISBN 978 0 7494 6520 9

Typeset by Saxon Graphics Ltd, Derby
Print production managed by Jellyfish
Printed and bound by CPI Group (UK) Ltd, Croydon, CR0 4YY

CONTENTS

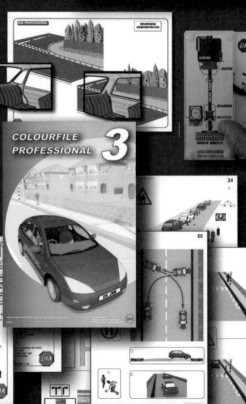

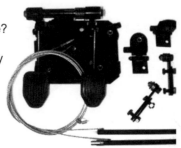

The sharpest minds need the finest advice. **Kogan Page** creates success.

www.koganpage.com

You are reading one of the thousands of books published by **Kogan Page**. As Europe's leading independent business book publishers **Kogan Page** has always sought to provide up-to-the-minute books that offer practical guidance at affordable prices.

KoganPage

INTRODUCTION

To be allowed to work professionally as a driving instructor you need to register with the Driving Standards Agency (DSA) as an Approved Driving Instructor (ADI).

You are not allowed to charge for driving instruction in a car unless your name is on the Register of ADIs or you hold a Licence to Give Instruction (trainee licence).

Registration with the DSA involves taking three separate parts of an exam – theory, own driving and instructional ability.

There are also several pre-entry qualifications. To apply for entry to the Register you must:

- hold a full UK or European unrestricted driving licence;
- have held the licence for at least four years out of the previous six years;
- not have been disqualified from driving at any time in the previous four years;
- be a 'fit and proper person'; this usually entails obtaining a Criminal Records Disclosure;
- pass the qualifying exams and register with the DSA within 12 months of doing so;
- meet current restrictions on accompanying a learner driver – ie minimum age 21 and have held a full licence for at least three years.

Notes on pre-entry qualifications:

- A foreign licence, a licence for a car with automatic transmission or a provisional licence held after passing the driving test all count towards the four years.
- Any convictions – whether they are for motoring or non-motoring offences – are usually taken into account.

The ADI Register

The Register was introduced as a compulsory qualification in 1970. Its main function is 'to maintain and improve the standard of car driving instruction available to the public. It ensures that the public can rely upon an acceptable minimum standard of tuition from registered instructors.'

Application

To make a start on your application you should obtain the starter pack from the DSA. The pack contains complete information about the exams and the qualifying process as well as an application form.

The pack can be ordered:

- by calling the DSA ADI service line on 0300 123 1126;
- or online at www.business link.gov.uk.

Before submitting your application you will normally need to obtain a Criminal Record Disclosure (CRD). Full details of how to do this are in the pack. However, your application may be affected if:

- you have endorsements on your licence;
- you have a disability or you have special needs;
- you have not held a full UK or EU licence for the full four years.

The DSA uses a contractor – TMG CRB – for all criminal records checks. For your first application you need to telephone TMG CRB on 0845 251 5000 to answer a few eligibility questions. You will then be given guidance on how to obtain the Disclosure.

Northern Ireland

To apply to become an ADI in Northern Ireland you should contact the DVA at:

Register of Approved Driving Instructors
DVA Testing
66 Balmoral Road
BELFAST
BT12 6QL
Tel: 028 9054 7933
www.dvtani.gov.uk/adi

Driving instruction as a career

Working as a driving instructor requires a great deal of concentration throughout the working day as you will be responsible for the safety of your pupils, other road users and yourself in busy road conditions.

The qualifying process is quite time consuming, relatively expensive and demands a high standard of knowledge and skills in both driving and instructing.

The whole process of training and taking the exams can usually take several months (even if you pass all three parts at the first attempt) and the pass rates are generally quite low (see later in this Introduction).

Having qualified as an ADI you will then be running your own business – either as a franchisee or as an independent instructor – and will need to generate a regular flow of customers and be able to compete with other instructors in your local area. However, the rewards are considerable: you will be working with a wide variety of people and will be giving them a valuable skill for life. Some of the benefits of being a self-employed ADI include the ability to organize your own work schedule to suit your individual requirements and the satisfaction of knowing that you are starting new young drivers on the road to safe driving.

To do the job thoroughly you will need good communication skills, patience, the ability to teach, and business sense.

Personal qualities

The DSA have suggested that, to be an effective driver trainer, you must:

- be patient, inspire confidence, and be tolerant of the mistakes of your clients;
- be an effective communicator, capable of using different methods of communication according to the needs of individual clients;
- be aware of the importance of feedback from clients in sustaining and improving levels of delivery;
- be positive, good natured and sympathetic in relations with others, especially with regard to working with others;
- show a proper concern for the safety and well-being of yourself, clients, passengers and other road users;
- be willing to continually reassess your needs in relation to current practice and future development and training.

Apart from your personal qualities you also need to be professional and knowledgeable.

Instructor qualities and attributes

Responsibilities

As a professional driver trainer you will have certain responsibilities, including:

- showing proper concern for the safety of your passengers, other road users and yourself;
- an awareness of the need to drive in an economical and environmentally friendly manner;
- being aware of the need for the safety and well-being of your pupils, particularly in the early stages of their training.

Concentration

You will need to have a high level of concentration throughout the working day. As a driver, remember that any distraction from the driving task can be potentially dangerous in today's traffic conditions. More particularly, as an instructor, your concentration is even more important. Read the road well ahead so that you can keep your pupils safe and relaxed and ready to learn.

Anticipation and awareness

As an experienced driver you will already appreciate that predicting what might happen as well as what is actually happening is an important element of driving. As an instructor, you will need to be even more aware of potential hazards in good time so that your pupil can prepare for them. Make sure you plan ahead as far as possible and anticipate potential hazards so that you can allow plenty of time for your instructions and for the pupil to respond appropriately.

You must recognize the needs of each individual pupil and anticipate how each of them might respond to changing situations.

Patience

An efficient and effective instructor shows patience and tolerance towards other road users. Displaying a positive attitude will set a good example to your pupils and help with their driver development. From a professional point of view, demonstrating tolerance and patience, not only with the pupil but also towards other road users, will help build your pupils' confidence in you and your ability as a professional driver trainer.

Confidence

As an instructor, it is important that you are confident in your own ability both as a driver and in the skills required to help you build your pupils' own confidence.

With your driver training, make sure you avoid any road or traffic situations that the pupil is not ready for so that you help them gradually build up confidence in their own ability.

Knowledge

As a professional driver trainer, you will need to have a sound knowledge of the rules and regulations in *The Highway Code* and *The Official DSA Guide to Driving* and the ability to pass on this knowledge so that your pupils will be able to apply the same principles to their own driving.

Make sure you keep up to date with any changes to the rules, regulations or legislation so that you are able to:

- handle your vehicle sympathetically and in an eco-friendly manner;
- apply modern coaching techniques;
- maintain a safe learning environment;
- offer advice to pupils on driver licensing requirements, basic mechanical principles, and the rules for safe driving on all types of road;
- answer pupils' questions confidently and competently.

Communication

As a driver you communicate your intentions to other road users in a variety of different ways by the correct use of indicators and arm signals, brake lights, early positioning, reversing lights, horn, flashing headlights, hazard warning flashers and eye contact.

Similarly, as an instructor your instruction skills will involve communicating effectively and in different ways with the wide variety of types of pupil you will be dealing with. Adapt the terminology you use so that all of your pupils understand exactly what you mean.

Communicate with your pupils by:

- establishing the level of understanding of the individual pupil;
- finding the most effective method and style of communication;
- explaining new principles in a clear and straightforward way;
- using visual aids effectively;
- giving practical demonstrations where appropriate;
- developing confidence and success in the pupil by using 'talk through' where necessary;
- giving directional instructions clearly and in good time;
- giving encouragement through positive feedback and praise where deserved;
- asking appropriate questions;
- encouraging the pupil to ask questions.

Awareness

New drivers need to be taught to a high standard, with hazard awareness playing an important part in their development. Teach your pupils to:

- handle the vehicle sympathetically and in an environmentally friendly way;
- drive with courtesy and consideration;
- look and plan well ahead, anticipating what might happen;
- take early action to avoid problems;
- compensate for other drivers' mistakes;
- understand what they are doing and why they are doing it.

Training for the exams

As well as the Register of ADIs, the DSA operates the 'Official Register of Driving Instructor Trainers' (ORDIT). This register is a list of trainers and training organizations who have been inspected by the DSA and who have achieved the minimum standard of training facilities. The Register can be found at www.direct.gov.uk.

You are not legally obliged to take a formal course of training but you may find it difficult to achieve the standard required – particularly for the practical exams – without some form of structured training with someone who specializes in driving instructor training.

ORDIT is a voluntary register; this means that not all training organizations and trainers are included. For various reasons, many very good trainers have decided not to join the Register.

The most important point about selecting a trainer is to try to speak to someone who has successfully trained with the trainer or organization. Recommendation is always a much more reliable indicator than any advert or publicity material. Ideally, try to find a fully qualified, experienced trainer who works independently, but if you do decide to opt for a larger organization or one of the nationally advertised schemes, make sure you find out if the course is suitable for your own particular needs.

To help you select a trainer or a course, the DSA suggest that you should ask a few important questions before signing up or committing yourself to a particular course. For example:

About the training

- *What is the full cost of the training, how long will it take and what are the terms and conditions?*
  The standard terms and conditions should be provided in writing for you to take away and read thoroughly before you commit yourself. The documentation should include any relevant agreements and commitments for both you and the provider.

- *Will I be given an assessment of my suitability to become an ADI?*
  You need an accurate assessment of whether you are suited to the job. Too many training organizations will simply take on any trainees who are willing to pay.

  Remember that the person interviewing you is not judging whether you are suitable as an instructor. They are trying to sell their services to you.

  Buying training is no different from anything else you buy – just make sure you know what you are committing yourself to.

- *Do the fees include the cost of the exams and any study materials?*
  These two items can add a considerable amount to the overall cost (probably about £300 for the exams and another £150 for books and other materials).

- *Does the course address my particular needs?*
  Find out what the course includes and whether it is suitable to your needs. For example, whether the training can be spread over a period of time or whether it is concentrated at specific times.

- *What extra support would I get if I fail any of the exams?*
  If, for example, you were to fail either of the practical exams on two occasions you would probably need extra, intensive tutoring to avoid the risk of failing at your third and final attempt.

- *Will it cost more if I need extra attempts?*
  Find out the cost of any extra training and have it confirmed in writing.

- *What if I find that I need more training?*
  Check on what extra costs you might have over and above the cost of the training. Travel costs and overnight accommodation can add considerably to your overall costs.

- *Will there be other trainees in the car for the practical training?*
  It is normal practice to have two trainees in the car to maximize the amount of in-car training time. Three to one is usually not advisable as it can be uncomfortable and confusing.

- *Does the course assume that I will need a trainee licence, even if this might be impractical for me?*
  Most trainee instructors find that they are able to pass the exams without the need for a trainee licence, but only if the training programme is properly structured.
     Details of the trainee licence are in Chapter 6.

- *Will the training take longer if I combine the training with my existing job?*
  Be careful about taking out a trainee licence – you would probably have to give up your existing employment, which puts you at risk of being without a job if you do not pass all three parts of the exam in the required period.

- *Will I be able to carry on with my existing job while training?*
  Generally you will need to take at least some time off during the working week, but the course should be flexible enough to allow you to fit it in with your work schedules and your individual requirements. Be wary of giving up your regular employment before you have qualified.

- *What is the refund policy?*
  For example, would you be able to obtain a refund if you failed the exams or were unable to complete the course, particularly if it is for reasons outside your control?

- *Is there provision for me to pay in instalments or stages?*
  Try to avoid paying for the complete course in advance. Ideally, pay for the training as you need it – it may cost a little more this way, but at least you are likely to lose less money if you have to pull out. You may find that you need to stagger your training to suit your existing work and the three parts of the exam.
     In an extreme case, if you fail the Part 2 exam on three attempts you would not be able to continue on to the Part 3 test and would lose the benefit of any Part 3 training.

- *What guarantee is there that there will be a suitable driving school willing to take me on as a trainee at the appropriate time? And will the driving school be able to provide me with sufficient pupils?*
  Some companies guarantee to give you a job at the end of your training or as a trainee under licence. Be careful. A 'job' usually means that you pay a weekly or monthly fee to be attached to the school, with no guarantee of a flow of pupils.

After you qualify

- *Will I be offered work as a franchised instructor? If so, what am I likely to earn and what will I have to pay?*
  When you are offered a 'job' this is really an opportunity to spend money with the company by buying a franchise with them. Remember that you will probably have to rent a car from them as part of the deal, so make sure you will have plenty of customers to use it.

  Try to find out how many instructors are working in your local area, how many instructors are working for the franchisor and whether you can contact any of them to get more information about the franchise.

- *What is the likely market for pupils in my local area?*
  You can often check on what is happening in your area by chatting to instructors at the local test centre or by contacting an instructor who might have taught a colleague or relative.

- *What will my start-up costs be?*

- *Would I be tied to the school for a fixed period?*

- *If I leave the school for any reason, would there be any restrictions on my starting up on my own account?*

- *Are there any grants available to cover the cost of my training or start-up?*
  You would not normally expect to pay any start-up fees – it is more usual to simply pay a weekly or monthly amount. Check the terms and conditions of the franchise to find out if these fees are payable in advance or arrears. Make sure you understand the restrictions that might apply if you decide to leave the school and whether there is a minimum fixed period. You may find, for example, that there are penalties for leaving without sufficient notice or within a particular period after starting with the company.

  The training organization or franchisor should be able to supply you with up-to-date information about any loans or grants that are available.

Training to become an ADI can be reasonably straightforward if you find the right trainer. On the other hand it can be quite stressful and time consuming if you do not prepare yourself properly from the start.

Remember that the pass rates for the ADI exams are quite low. The DSA published figures for 2010/11 were:

Part 1 – theory: 47 per cent;

Part 2 – own driving: 40 per cent;

Part 3 – instructional ability: 34 per cent.

During this particular year, nearly 12,000 people applied to start the qualifying process, but only about 4,000 actually qualified as ADIs.

Cost of training

A realistic figure for the cost of training is usually around £3,000, but this will vary, depending on what kind of training you take and whether you decide to take out a trainee licence.

Although this will be the bulk of your costs, you need to add in the cost of the exams and registration. At the present time (January 2012) these are:

Part 1 – theory and hazard perception test: £90;

Part 2 – practical own driving test: £111;

Trainee licence (if required): £140;

Part 3 – instructional ability: £111;

Initial registration (and every four years): £300.

In Northern Ireland the fees are:

Part 1: £72;

Part 2: £130;

Trainee licence: £120;

Part 3: £138;

Registration/renewal: £240.

For up to date details of all fees, check with www.businesslink.gov.uk or www.dvtani.gov.uk

The ADI exams

01

T he qualifying exam for registration is in three parts:

Part 1 – theory test. Multiple-choice questions followed by a hazard perception test.

Part 2 – driving technique. Eyesight test followed by practical driving.

Part 3 – instructional ability. A practical test of your ability to give instruction.

You must take the exams in order and must complete all three parts within two years of passing the theory test.

You are allowed an unlimited number of attempts at the theory test, but for the practical tests there is a limit of three attempts for each part.

If you are not able to pass either of the practical tests within three attempts you must wait until the end of the two-year period before starting the whole process again. This means that you would have to take and pass the Part 1 test again before moving on to another attempt at the practical tests.

If you run out of time and have not passed all three parts within the two years you would have go through the whole process again, starting with the theory test.

Details of each part of the qualifying exams are given in later chapters – Chapter 2 for the Part 1 (theory test), Chapter 4 for the Part 2 (own driving test) and Chapter 7 for the Part 3 (instructional ability test).

Exam fees and qualification costs

There is a fee for each part of the exam:

Part 1 – theory test: £90;

Part 2 – own driving test: £111;

Part 3 – instructional ability test: £111.

Other fees connected to the cost of qualifying include:

trainee licence (for full details of the trainee licence, see Chapter 6): £140;

registration fee (for a period of four years): £300.

These are the costs in early 2012, but for up-to-date fees check www. businesslink.gov.uk/dsafees or phone the DSA on 0300 200 1122.

The cost of training is likely to add a further £2,500– £3,000 or so to the above costs depending on whether you decide on taking a full structured course with one of the national training organizations or whether you organize your own ad hoc training locally.

Qualification

As outlined earlier, to qualify for taking the exams you must:

- hold a British or Northern Ireland car driving licence or hold a European Union (EU) or European Economic Area (EEA) licence;
- have held that licence for a total of four years out of the past six years prior to entering the Register after qualifying. A foreign driving licence, automatic car driving licence or a provisional licence held after passing the driving test all count towards the four years;
- not have been disqualified from driving at any time in the four years prior to applying to enter the register;
- Be a 'fit and proper' person to have your name entered on the Register.

All three parts of the exam are quite stringent, but particularly the practical exams. This is illustrated by the fact that the pass rates for the exams are very low.

For 2010/11 the official figures published by the DSA were:

Part 1 – theory test: 47 per cent;

Part 2 – driving: 48 per cent;

Part 3 – instructional ability: 34 per cent.

From these figures, and bearing in mind that you are only allowed a maximum of three attempts at each part of the practical exams, it is clear you should make sure that you are properly prepared by taking structured training from a qualified and experienced instructor trainer.

Although the syllabus for each part of the practical tests is included in Chapters 4 and 7 there is no substitute for effective, practical, in-car training – preferably on a one-to-one basis.

The examiner

All the examiners on the practical tests are specially selected and trained for the job of assessing instructors rather than learner drivers. A team of about 50 or so senior examiners ('driver training assessment managers') conducts the tests at centres around the UK.

Standards

Part 1

The test is in two parts: a multiple-choice question paper followed by a hazard perception test.

For the multiple-choice part of the test you are required to answer 100 questions within 90 minutes. The pass mark for this part is 85 per cent, but you must also achieve a minimum of 80 per cent in each of the subject 'bands'. The purpose of the banding is to check whether you have sufficient knowledge spread over the complete syllabus. The questions are designed to test your knowledge of:

- the Highway Code;
- the rules of the road;
- your knowledge of instructional techniques.

Details of the banding system and the complete syllabus are in Chapter 2, with a selection of official DSA practice questions in Chapter 3 and a mock test using non-DSA questions in Chapter 9.

Hazard perception test (HPT)

This part of the test is designed to check on your ability to recognize and identify the types of hazard that you will come across in normal driving. The HPT consists of 14 video clips, each lasting about one minute. By using a mouse button you can respond to each hazard as it appears on the screen. The earlier you click, the more points you score.

There are 15 scoreable hazards and you can obtain a maximum of 5 for each hazard. Out of the total of 75 you need a score of 57 to pass.

Part 2

This part of the exam assesses your own driving. It is not simply a longer version of the L test – it is an advanced driving test. To quote the DSA:

A very high standard of competence is required. You must show that you have a thorough knowledge of the principles of good driving and road safety and that you can apply them in practice.

You are allowed a maximum of six 'driving faults' – minor errors – with no 'serious' or 'dangerous' faults. Your preparation for this part of the exam should cover all the set manoeuvres and a wide variety of road and traffic conditions, including urban and rural roads, dual carriageways and motorways where possible.

At the start of the test you will be asked a few questions on basic vehicle safety. For some of these questions you will be asked by the examiner to 'show me' and for others 'tell me'.

During the test the examiner will be assessing you on all the following subjects:

- expert handling of the controls;
- use of correct road procedure;
- anticipation of the actions of other road users and the taking of appropriate action;
- sound judgement of distance, speed and timing;
- consideration for the convenience and safety of other road users;
- driving in an environmentally friendly manner.

More detail on the Part 2 test is in Chapter 4.

Part 3

In the Part 3 exam the examiner will act as a learner driver at different stages of learning. The test lasts about an hour and is split into two 'phases'. For the first phase the examiner will role play a learner at an early stage of training, with the second phase involving a learner who is at or about test stage (or a qualified driver requiring refresher training).

You will be tested on three main subject areas:

- core competencies;
- instructional techniques;
- instructor's characteristics.

The syllabus for this part of the exam consists of:

- safety precautions on entering the car and explanation of the controls;
- moving off and making normal stops;
- driving the vehicle backwards and while doing so entering limited openings to the right or left;
- turning the vehicle round in the road to face the opposite direction using forward and reverse gears;
- parking close to the kerb using reverse gears;
- practical instruction in how to use mirrors and how to make an emergency stop;

- approaching and turning corners;
- judgement of speed and general road positioning;
- dealing with coming out onto T junctions;
- dealing with all aspects of road crossroads;
- dealing with pedestrian crossings and giving appropriate signals by using your indicator and your arm in a clear and unmistakable manner;
- meeting and crossing the path of and overtaking other vehicles including allowing enough clearance, to include following distance for other road users.

During the test the examiner will stay 'in role' as much as possible. You should treat them as you would a genuine pupil.

The examiner assesses you on the method, accuracy and clarity of your instruction for each of the nominated subjects.

More detail on the Part 3 exam is in Chapter 7.

Disabilities

If you have a disability you can apply for the ADI exams under special regulations, depending on your individual circumstances:

1 If you have a driving licence that restricts you to driving a car with automatic transmission because of your disability, you can apply for the ADI registration. The exams will be exactly the same as for other candidates, except that you are allowed to take the practical tests in a car with automatic transmission.

   Before your application can be considered, you would need to have an assessment of your ability to take control of the car from the passenger seat where appropriate or necessary. To apply, first contact the DSA, who will advise where you can take the assessment, after which you will be issued with an 'Emergency Control Certificate' (ECC). The certificate will indicate what additional controls on the car, if any, will be needed. You then submit the certificate with your application for registration.

   After taking the exam and having qualified, your ADI certificate will show that you are restricted in giving instruction in a car with automatic transmission and whether any additional controls are required.

2 The ADI regulations allow for someone who has a disability and who holds a full licence for manual transmission cars to obtain registration provided that they have an ECC issued. The ECC will determine what extra controls are needed to overcome the disability and the ADI certificate will be amended accordingly.

Trainee licence

Once you have passed the first two parts of the qualifying exam you are eligible to take out a trainee licence. This licence enables you to give driving instruction professionally while preparing for the third part of the exam – the instructional ability test.

It is not essential to take out a trainee licence, but it is a means of gaining valuable work experience with genuine pupils before taking the final part of the exam.

There are several restrictions to having a trainee licence, including the need to be supervised for part of your lesson time. There is also a cost involved – £140 as at January 2012. Licences are issued for only six months and a further licence is only granted by the Registrar under exceptional circumstances.

Full details of the trainee licence are in Chapter 6, but note that there are proposals by the DSA to change the requirements for a trainee licence or to abolish the trainee system completely. A consultation exercise on these proposals is expected sometime during 2012.

ADI Part 1 – theory test

02

The theory test is the first of the three-part qualifying exam for the ADI Register.

Once you have passed this part of the exam you have a maximum of two years in which to pass the other parts of the exam. There is no limit to the number of times you can take this part of the exam. (In Northern Ireland you are allowed only three attempts in a two-year period).

The test is in two parts – a multiple-choice question paper followed by an on-screen hazard perception test. Both parts of the test are taken on the same occasion and both parts must be passed in order to have an overall pass.

The test is available in English and Welsh.

Questions for the test are based on:

- principles of road safety generally and their application in particular circumstances;
- techniques of driving a car correctly, safely and courteously;
- understanding and application of vehicle control and road procedure;
- recognizing hazards and taking proper action;
- dealing correctly with pedestrians and other road users;
- use of safety equipment;
- theory and practice of learning, teaching and assessment;
- instructional techniques needed to teach a pupil to drive a car;
- the correction of a pupil's errors;
- knowledge of the appropriate manner and relationship between instructor and pupil;
- a simple understanding of vehicle adaptations for drivers with a disability;

- *The Highway Code;*
- the DSA publications *The Official DSA Guide to Driving – the essential skills* and *The Official DSA Guide to Learning to Drive;*
- interpretation of the reasons for failure given in the DSA form DL25A – the driving test report;
- knowledge, adequate for the needs of driving instruction, of the mechanics and design of a car.

To help you prepare for the Part 1 exam the DSA has compiled a list of books and other material that will assist you in your studies:

- *The Official Highway Code;*
- *The Official DSA Guide to Learning to Drive;*
- *The Official DSA Guide to Driving – the essential skills;*
- *Helping Learners to Practise – the official guide;*
- *Know your Traffic Signs;*
- 'The Official DSA Guide to Hazard Perception' DVD;
- 'Prepare for your Practical Test' DVD;
- D100 leaflet – 'What you need to know about your driving licence';
- *Instructional Techniques and Practices for Driving Instructors;*
- *The Driving Instructor's Handbook;*
- *Practical Teaching Skills for Driving Instructors.*

Booking your theory test

You can book online, by phone or by post.

Online. If you use this method you will be able to obtain a time and date for your test immediately. Book online at www.direct.gov.uk.

By phone. Call 0870 0101 372. For Welsh speakers the number is 0870 0100 372.

For bookings online or by phone you will need your driving licence number and credit or debit card details. You will be given a booking confirmation number straightaway and should receive an official confirmation letter within a week or so.

By post. Fill in the application form that is given to you with the starter pack. You can expect to receive an appointment letter within about 10 days or so.

In Northern Ireland application for the theory test must be made by post. The appropriate forms can be obtained from DVTA at 66 Balmoral Road, Belfast BT12 6QL or by phoning 028 9054 7933. After you have sent off the forms the DVTA will carry out various security checks on you and then issue a personal reference number.

At this stage you can then phone the theory test line on 0845 600 6700 to book an appointment. You can expect to receive a confirmation appointment letter within 10 days or so.

Fees. The fee for the Part 1 ADI exam is currently £90 (January 2012). In Northern Ireland the fee is £72.

Theory test centres. Part 1 ADI tests are held at centres across the country. These locations are listed in Appendix IV.

Dates for the test are usually shown in local driving test centres and can also be found on the DSA website.

Special needs

The DSA try to ensure that the test is accessible to all candidates.

If you have special needs you should give as much information as possible at the time of booking so that appropriate arrangements can be made.

A voiceover – in English or Welsh – is available if you have reading difficulties or dyslexia. (This facility is not currently available in Northern Ireland.)

Candidates with special needs can ask for extra time to complete the test. The application must be supported by evidence such as a letter from an employer, trainer or doctor.

If you would have difficulty in using a computer mouse because of a physical disability it is possible to have special arrangements to use a different method, particularly for the hazard perception test which follows the multiple-choice part of the test. Again, this should be stated at the time of booking the test.

Multiple-choice questions

These questions are designed to test your knowledge and understanding of:

- *The Highway Code;*
- rules of the road;
- instructional techniques.

You are allowed 90 minutes to answer a total of 100 questions. The questions are split into four bands to ensure that all candidates are tested on their knowledge and understanding across the whole of the syllabus.

Band 1:
   - road procedure (25 questions).

Band 2:
   - traffic signs and signals (5 questions);

- car control (10 questions);
- pedestrians (5 questions);
- mechanical knowledge (5 questions).

Band 3:
- driving tests (10 questions);
- disabilities (5 questions);
- law (10 questions).

Band 4:
- publications (10 questions);
- instructional techniques (15 questions).

Most questions have four alternative choices with only one correct answer, but some have more alternatives with a requirement to give two or more correct answers.

Only one question at a time is shown on the screen and you can move backwards or forwards through the questions. If you want to recheck any of your answers you can go back to them and make any alterations as required. You would also be alerted by the system if you had not answered a question completely.

The overall pass mark for this part of the test is 85 per cent – that is, you must answer correctly 85 of the 100 questions. You must also have a minimum of 80 per cent (20 out of 25) correct answers in each of the four bands.

This means that you could possibly fail the test with an overall pass mark of more than 85 per cent, but with less than the 80 per cent requirement in one or more of the four bands.

Example questions

These questions are reproduced under the terms of Crown Copyright.

Note: mark one answer unless otherwise indicated.

Band 1: Road procedure

1.1 A pelican crossing that crosses the road in a straight line and has a central island must be treated as:

- one crossing in daylight only.
- one complete crossing.
- two separate crossings.
- two crossings during darkness.

The lights that control the crossing show to both directions of traffic. If a pedestrian from either side is still crossing when the amber light is flashing, you must wait.

1.2 You wish to overtake a long, slow-moving vehicle on a busy road.
You should:

- follow it closely and keep moving out to see the road ahead.
- flash your headlights for the oncoming traffic to give way.
- stay behind until the driver waves you past.
- keep well back until you can see that it is clear.

If you wish to overtake a long vehicle, stay well back so that you can see the
road ahead. *Don't*:

- get up close to the vehicle – this will restrict your view of the road
  ahead.
- get impatient – overtaking on a busy road calls for sound judgement.
- take a gamble – only overtake when you can see that you can safely
  complete the manoeuvre.

1.3 You have been involved in an argument before starting your journey.
This has made you feel angry. You should:

- start to drive, but open a window.
- drive slower than normal and turn your radio on.
- have an alcoholic drink to help you relax before driving.
- calm down before you start to drive.

If you are feeling upset or angry you should wait until you have calmed
down before setting out on a journey.

1.4 You think the driver of the vehicle in front has forgotten to cancel the
right indicator. You should:

- flash your lights to alert the driver.
- sound your horn before overtaking.
- overtake on the left if there is room.
- stay behind and not overtake.

The driver may be unsure of the location of a junction and turn suddenly. Be
cautious and don't attempt to overtake.

1.5 A driver pulls out of a side road in front of you. You have to brake
hard. You should:

- ignore the error and stay calm.
- flash your lights to show your annoyance.
- sound your horn to show your annoyance.
- overtake as soon as possible.

Where there are a number of side roads, be alert. Be especially careful if
there are a lot of parked vehicles because they can make it more difficult for
drivers emerging to see you. Try to be tolerant if a vehicle does emerge and
you have to brake quickly. Don't react aggressively.

1.6 You are in a line of traffic. The driver behind you is following very closely. What action should you take?

- ignore the following driver and continue to drive within the speed limit.
- slow down, gradually increasing the gap between you and the vehicle in front.
- signal left and wave the following driver past.
- move over to a position just left of the centre line of the road.

It can be worrying to see that the car behind is following you too closely. Give yourself a greater safety margin by easing back from the vehicle in front.

1.7 What action would you take when elderly people are crossing the road?

- wave them across so they know that you have seen them.
- be patient and allow them to cross in their own time.
- rev the engine to let them know that you are waiting.
- tap the horn in case they are hard of hearing.

Be aware that elderly people might take a long time to cross the road. They might also be hard of hearing and not hear you approaching. Don't hurry elderly people across the road by getting too close to them or revving your engine.

1.8 There is a slow-moving vehicle ahead of you. You are unsure what the driver is going to do. You should:

- pass on the left.
- pass on the right.
- stay behind.
- move closer.

When a vehicle is travelling slowly the driver or rider is probably looking for a turning or entrance. Be patient and stay behind them. They are quite likely to change direction or stop, probably without signalling.

1.9 You are waiting to emerge left from a minor road. A large vehicle is approaching from the right. You have time to turn but should wait because the large vehicle:

- can easily hide an overtaking vehicle.
- can turn suddenly.
- is difficult to steer in a straight line.
- can easily hide vehicles from the left.

Large vehicles can hide other vehicles that are overtaking, especially motorcycles which may be filtering past queuing traffic. You need to be aware of the possibility of hidden vehicles and not assume that it is safe to emerge.

1.10 Some two-way roads are divided into three lanes. These are particularly dangerous because traffic in both directions:

- − can use the middle lane to overtake.
- − can travel faster in poor weather conditions.
- − can overtake on the left.
- − uses the middle lane for emergencies only.

If you intend to overtake you must consider that approaching traffic could be planning the same manoeuvre. When you have considered the situation and have decided it is safe, indicate your intentions early. This will show the approaching traffic that you intend to pull out. Some of these roads have solid white lines marked to allow for overtaking in one direction only, usually for uphill traffic.

Band 2: Traffic signs and signals

2.1 What colour are the reflective studs between a motorway and its slip road?

- − amber.
- − white.
- − green.
- − red.

The studs between the carriageway and the hard shoulder are normally red. These change to green where there is a slip road. They will help you identify slip roads when visibility is poor or when it is dark.

2.2 Yellow lines across the road on the approach to roundabouts are to:

- − help you choose the right lane.
- − help you to keep the correct separation distance.
- − make you aware of your speed.
- − tell you the distance to the roundabout.

Yellow lines across the road on the approach to roundabouts are to make drivers aware of their speed.

Car control

2.3 Why should you *not* coast downhill?

- − it causes more wear and tear on the tyres.
- − fuel consumption will increase.
- − you have less control of your vehicle.
- − it causes more wear and tear on the suspension.

When travelling downhill the engine can act as a brake to help control your speed. If you coast, then engine braking is lost and it may be more difficult to keep control especially on a long hill where the brakes may overheat and lose efficiency.

2.4   Your car starts to skid and the rear wheels are sliding to the left. You should:
- steer to the left.
- steer to the right.
- not steer at all.
- apply your handbrake.

Looking well ahead and driving according to the road conditions should prevent this happening in the first place. Once a skid has started your vehicle is out of control; this is highly dangerous for you and others. When the rear wheels start to skid, try to steer in the same direction. If the rear goes left, steer left, if it goes right, steer right. Be careful not to over steer too far, otherwise you will skid in the opposite direction.

2.5   When reversing a car in a straight line you:
- must hold the steering wheel with both hands.
- may steer with one hand if this helps.
- must keep your hands at the 'ten to two' position.
- must keep your hands at the 'quarter to three' position.

It is normal for a driver to steer with both hands when reversing. However, it is permissible to use one hand to steer when reversing provided there is no apparent loss of control.

2.6   If the power fails on a power-assisted steering system this will result in:
- locking the steering mechanism.
- more effort needed to turn the steering wheel.
- an increase in tyre wear.
- less effort to turn the steering wheel.

Much more effort will be required if the system fails. Most power steering systems only work when the ignition is switched on.

Pedestrians

2.7   At a toucan crossing:
- there is no flashing amber light.
- cyclists are not permitted.
- there is a continuously flashing amber beacon.
- you only stop if someone is waiting to cross.

There are some crossings where cycle routes lead the cyclists to cross at the same place as pedestrians. These are called toucan crossings. Always look out for cyclists, as they're likely to be approaching faster than pedestrians.

2.8 You see a pedestrian with a white stick and red band. This means that the person is:

- physically disabled.
- deaf only.
- blind only.
- deaf and blind.

If someone is deaf as well as blind, they may be carrying a white stick with a red reflective band. You can't see if a pedestrian is deaf. Don't assume everyone can hear you approaching.

Mechanical knowledge

2.9 Catalytic converters are fitted to make the:

- engine produce more power.
- exhaust system easier to replace.
- engine run quietly.
- exhaust fumes cleaner.

Harmful gases in the exhaust system pollute the atmosphere. These gases are reduced by up to 90 per cent if a catalytic converter is fitted. Cleaner air benefits everyone, especially people who live or work near congested roads.

Band 3: Driving test

3.1 During the driving test a candidate makes a smooth direct gear change from fourth to second gear. The examiner observing this action would assess this as being:

- satisfactory.
- a driving fault.
- poor use of gears.
- a serious fault.

It is perfectly acceptable to miss out gears and select the appropriate gear for the situation. Always ensure that the road speed matches the engine speed for the gear required.

3.2 At the start of a driving test a candidate finds that their inertia reel seat belt has temporarily locked and they cannot put it on. They should:

- carry on with the test without a seat belt.
- ask the examiner to postpone the test and seek a further appointment.
- put it on as soon as the belt is released.
- ignore it and fit it sometime later.

There are exemptions provided in the regulations. If an inertia reel seat belt has temporarily locked because the vehicle is parked on a gradient, the driver may move the vehicle. As soon as the mechanism has unlocked and released itself, the driver should stop and apply the belt.

Disabilities

3.3 A person who is blind in one eye is:
- only permitted to drive while wearing glasses.
- required to have a restricted licence to drive a motor car.
- permitted to drive a motor car.
- not permitted to drive a motor car.

A person who has only one eye is not considered to have a disability and will be given a normal licence to drive a motor car.

Law

3.4 You leave your vehicle overnight on a road with a 40 mph speed limit. You should park:
- facing the traffic.
- with parking lights on.
- with dipped headlights on.
- near a street light.

Make sure that other road users can see you. Park in the direction of the traffic flow so that you aren't mistaken for a moving vehicle.

3.5 You are not allowed to travel in the right-hand lane of a three-lane motorway, if you are driving a:
- small delivery van.
- motorcycle.
- vehicle towing a trailer.
- motorcycle and sidecar.

A vehicle with a trailer is restricted to 60 mph. For this reason it is not allowed in the right-hand lane as it might hold up the faster-moving traffic that wishes to overtake in that lane.

3.6 It is a driver's responsibility to ensure that the front-seat passenger wears a seat belt if the passenger is under:
- 14 years old.
- 15 years old.
- 16 years old.
- 18 years old.

Seat belts save lives and reduce the risk of injury. It's your legal responsibility to ensure that all passengers under 14 years old wear a seat belt, or are fastened in an approved child restraint. However, it is good practice to ensure that all other passengers wear seat belts.

3.7 Learner drivers in a car must be supervised by someone who is:

- 18 (or over) and who has held a full licence for that category of vehicle for one year.
- 20 (or over) and has held a full licence for that category for three years.
- 21 (or over) and who has held a full licence for that category of vehicle for at least three years.
- 21 (or over) and who has held a full licence for that category of vehicle for at least one year.

A person who accompanies a learner must have held a full EC/EEA driving licence for at least three years and still hold one for the category of vehicle being used by the learner driver. The accompanying driver must be at least 21 years of age. All Approved Driving Instructors meet that criterion and many more.

Band 4: Publications

4.1 Which of these vehicles might you find using a flashing amber light on a dual carriageway?

- a non-emergency ambulance.
- an off-duty fire engine.
- an emergency doctor's vehicle.
- a disabled person's vehicle.

An amber flashing light on a vehicle indicates that it is slow-moving. Powered vehicles used by disabled people are limited to 8 mph. On dual carriageways they must display an amber flashing light.

4.2 Why are hatch markings painted in the centre of the road?

- to separate traffic flowing in opposite directions
- to mark an area to be used by overtaking motorcyclists
- to warn of a temporary marking for roadworks
- to show the area of a bus lane.

Hatched markings are painted at potentially dangerous areas to separate streams of traffic. Examples are at sharp bends or to protect traffic turning right.

Instructional techniques

4.3 To help a pupil attain a good standard of driving the amount of verbal instruction should be:

- maintained at the same level regardless of competence.
- increased as the test approaches.
- reduced as their competence increases.
- stopped when they reach test standard.

As a pupil's knowledge and ability increase, the amount of verbal instruction should be adjusted accordingly. It is important to reduce direct instruction and transfer appropriate responsibility as the pupil's ability increases.

4.4 As an aid to progressive learning a pupil's progress on a course should be measured:

- as an ongoing assessment.
- at the end of the course.
- only when an improvement has been made.
- when the pupil has reached a plateau.

Regular assessment and feedback are a two-way process. This will enable the instructor to adjust the level of content and style of development to suit the pupil's strengths and weaknesses.

4.5 The 'learning plateau' sometimes occurs during training. This refers to:

- a slowing down of the pace of instruction.
- a temporary halt in the learning process.
- a common difficulty experienced by some people in hand-to-eye coordination.
- pupils who have specific learning difficulties.

Learning is not always a continuous upward process. It is common for many pupils to reach a learning plateau. Once this level has been attained, further progress usually appears to come to a halt. After a short period of time most pupils will overcome this problem.

4.6 Learning by rote is an appropriate teaching method for:

- memorizing facts and figures.
- problem solving.
- teaching hazard perception.
- teaching coordination.

While there may be advantages in learning some subjects by rote, it is only a starting point on which to develop further understanding and practice. There are various methods that can be used when teaching someone to drive.

4.7   Having decided upon a lesson plan for a particular pupil, an instructor should:

- use the same plan every time the same exercise is covered in the future.
- keep strictly to the prepared plan.
- alter the lesson plan if necessary.
- only continue with the lesson plan if the pupil agrees.

The ADI should set out clear aims and objectives at the beginning of the lesson. However, this does not compel the instructor to stick to them regardless of the pupil's performance. An ADI should have a flexible approach to training. The pupil's needs are the priority when planning a lesson.

4.8   An instructor observes a driving fault committed by the pupil. This should be:

- used as a teaching point.
- used as a warning to the pupil.
- ignored and the lesson continued with.
- written down for later discussion.

Avoid retrospective comment and deal with the fault at the earliest opportunity. Use it as a teaching point to encourage a change for the better in the pupil.

Hazard perception test (HPT)

This is the second part of the theory test, consisting of a series of short video clips featuring different types of hazards.

The hazards depicted are normally ones that involve other vehicles, pedestrians and various road conditions and which would require some form of response from the driver such as changing speed or direction. The video clips are designed to test your ability to identify the type of hazard that you might encounter in normal driving.

As potential hazards appear on the screen you have to click the computer mouse promptly to indicate that you have spotted the hazard. The earlier you click, the more points you can score. It is really all about spotting and identifying a developing hazard as early as possible.

HPT pass mark

There are 14 video clips, with 15 scoreable hazards in total. You can score a maximum of five points on each hazard, making a total possible 75 marks.

The required pass mark is 57 out of 75.

To practise for the hazard perception test, various DVDs are available, including 'The Official Guide to Hazard Perception' from the DSA.

You must pass both parts of the test – multiple choice and HPT – on the same occasion.

Preparation for the test

When preparing for the ADI Part 1 test, make sure you are not tempted to skimp on your reading or rely solely on the brief explanation provided by the DSA. Avoid trying to memorize any of the questions or the correct answers. You cannot learn effectively or remember the answers to several hundred questions in this way.

To be able to answer the questions in the theory test without difficulty and to prepare for the Part 3 test, you need to have a thorough knowledge and understanding of the rules and principles involved.

At the test centre

Make sure you arrive at the test centre in good time so that you can prepare yourself properly.

You need to take with you your photo-card driving licence and the paper counterpart. If you still have the old-style paper licence you will also need to take your passport or some other form of visual identity.

At the start of the test, once your documents have been checked and processed, you will be allowed to work through a practice session to familiarize yourself with the computer system. If you have any difficulties or doubts, test centre staff are available to help.

The result

Theory test results are normally given to candidates before they leave the test centre. At the same time you will be given details of how to apply for the next part of the ADI exam – the test of your driving ability.

Next steps

After you have taken the theory test you will receive confirmation from the DSA of the result and an indication of the marks you obtained in each section. At the same time you will be given details about how to apply for the driving ability test. Remember that you have a maximum of two years from the date you passed the theory test in which to take and pass the practical exams.

If you fail either the multiple choice or the HPT you will need to take the complete test again.

Reading materials

For details of all suggested reading materials for the ADI exams, see Appendix II.

All these publications are available from DeskTop Driving; tel: 01903 882299 (www.desktopdriving.co.uk) and other suppliers, including DSA merchandising (0870 241 4523).

Part 1 questions – official DSA practice questions

03

The questions in this chapter are reproduced under the terms of Crown Copyright.

Please note: these are some of the official DSA practice questions. The explanations, which are shown in italics after the question, are the official wording as supplied by the DSA.

For a more detailed explanation you should refer to the appropriate reading material on pages 219–20 and not rely simply on the official text.

Mark one answer unless indicated otherwise.

Band 1 – Road procedure

1.1 On a road where trams operate, which of these vehicles will be most at risk from the tram rails?

- cars.
- cycles.
- buses.
- lorries.

The narrow wheels of a bicycle can become stuck in the tram rails, causing the cyclist to stop suddenly, wobble or even lose balance altogether. The tram lines are also slippery, which could cause a cyclist to slide or fall off.

1.2   The use of the horn is to:
- alert others to your presence.
- allow you right of way.
- greet other road users.
- signal your annoyance.

Your horn must not be used between 11.30 pm and 7.00 am in a built-up area or when you are stationary, unless a moving vehicle poses a danger. Its function is to alert other road users to your presence.

1.3   You are in a one-way street and want to turn right. You should position yourself:
- in the right-hand lane.
- in the left-hand lane.
- in either lane, depending on the traffic.
- just left of the centre line.

If you're travelling in a one-way street and wish to turn right you should take up a position in the right-hand lane. This will enable other road users not wishing to turn to proceed on the left. Indicate your intention and take up your position in good time.

1.4   You wish to turn right. You should take up the correct position in good time to:
- allow other drivers to pull out in front of you.
- give a better view into the road that you're joining.
- help other road users know what you intend to do.
- allow drivers to pass you on the right.

If you wish to turn right into a side road take up your position in good time. Move to the centre of the road when it's safe to do so. This will allow vehicles to pass you on the left. Early planning will show other traffic what you intend to do.

1.5   You are most likely to be affected by a side wind on:
- a narrow country lane.
- an open stretch of road.
- a busy stretch of road.
- a long, straight road.

In windy conditions, care must be taken on exposed roads. A strong gust of wind can blow you off course. Watch out for other road users who are particularly likely to be affected, such as:

- *cyclists;*
- *motorcyclists;*

- *high-sided lorries;*
- *vehicles towing trailers.*

1.6 In windy conditions you need to take extra care when:
- using the brakes.
- making a hill start.
- turning into a narrow road.
- passing pedal cyclists.

You should always give cyclists plenty of room when overtaking. When it's windy, a sudden gust could blow them off course.

1.7 You think the driver of the vehicle in front has forgotten to cancel the right indicator. You should:
- flash your lights to alert the driver.
- sound your horn before overtaking.
- overtake on the left if there is room.
- stay behind and not overtake.

The driver may be unsure of the location of a junction and turn suddenly. Be cautious and don't attempt to overtake.

1.8 At a blind junction you must stop:
- behind the line, then edge forward to see clearly.
- beyond the line at a point where you can see clearly.
- only if there is traffic on the main road.
- only if you are turning to the right.

The STOP sign has been put here because there is a poor view into the main road. You must stop because it will not be possible to assess the situation on the move, however slowly you are travelling.

1.9 A driver pulls out of a side road in front of you. You have to brake hard. You should:
- ignore the error and stay calm.
- flash your lights to show your annoyance.
- sound your horn to show your annoyance.
- overtake as soon as possible.

Where there are a number of side roads, be alert. Be especially careful if there are a lot of parked vehicles because they can make it more difficult for drivers emerging to see you. Try to be tolerant if a vehicle does emerge and you have to brake quickly. Don't react aggressively.

1.10 You are turning left at a junction. Pedestrians have started to cross the road. You should:

- – go on, giving them plenty of room.
- – stop and wave at them to cross.
- – blow your horn and proceed.
- – give way to them.

If you're turning into a side road, pedestrians already crossing the road have priority and you should give way to them.
 Don't:

- *wave them across the road;*
- *sound your horn;*
- *flash your lights;*
- *give any other misleading signal – other road users may misinterpret your signal and you might lead the pedestrian into a dangerous situation. If a pedestrian is slow or indecisive be patient and wait. Don't hurry them across by revving your engine.*

1.11 The left-hand lane on a three-lane motorway is for use by:

- – any vehicle.
- – large vehicles only.
- – emergency vehicles only.
- – slow vehicles only.

On a motorway all traffic should use the left-hand lane unless overtaking. Use the centre or right-hand lanes if you need to overtake. Make sure that you move back to the left-hand lane when you've finished overtaking. Don't stay in the middle or right-hand lane if the left-hand lane is free.

1.12 What is the right-hand lane used for on a three-lane motorway?

- – emergency vehicles only.
- – overtaking.
- – vehicles towing trailers.
- – coaches only.

You should keep to the left and only use the right-hand lane if you're passing slower-moving traffic.

1.13 On motorways you should never overtake on the left unless:

- you can see well ahead that the hard shoulder is clear.
- the traffic in the right-hand lane is signalling right.
- you warn drivers behind by signalling left.
- there is a queue of traffic to your right that is moving more slowly.

Only overtake on the left if traffic is moving slowly in queues and the traffic on your right is moving more slowly than the traffic in your lane.

1.14 You are travelling on a motorway. You decide you need a rest. You should:

- stop on the hard shoulder.
- leave by the next exit.
- park on the slip road.
- park on the central reservation.

You must not stop on a motorway, hard shoulder or slip road except in an emergency or traffic queue. You must stop when signalled to do so by a police officer, Highways Agency Traffic Officer (HATO) or traffic signals. Try to plan your journey so that you have regular rest stops.

1.15 You break down on a motorway. You need to call for help. Why may it be better to use an emergency roadside telephone rather than a mobile phone?

- it connects you to a local garage.
- using a mobile phone will distract other drivers.
- it allows easy location by the emergency services.
- mobile phones do not work on motorways.

On a motorway it is best to use a roadside emergency telephone so that the emergency services are able to locate you easily. The nearest telephone is indicated by an arrow on the marker posts at the edge of the hard shoulder. If you do use a mobile phone, the emergency services will want to know your exact location. Before you call, find out the number on the nearest marker post. This number will tell the emergency services your exact location.

1.16 After a breakdown you need to rejoin the main carriageway of a motorway from the hard shoulder. You should:
- move out onto the carriageway then build up your speed.
- move out onto the carriageway using your hazard lights.
- gain speed on the hard shoulder before moving out onto the carriageway.
- wait on the hard shoulder until someone flashes their headlights at you.

Wait for a safe gap in the traffic before you move out. Indicate your intention and use the hard shoulder to gain speed but don't force your way into the traffic.

1.17 A crawler lane on a motorway is normally found:
- on a gradient.
- before a service area.
- before a junction.
- along the hard shoulder.

Slow-moving, large vehicles might slow down the progress of other traffic. On a steep gradient this extra lane is provided for these slow-moving vehicles to allow the faster-moving traffic to flow more easily.

1.18 Where you see street lights but no speed limit signs the limit is usually:
- 30 mph.
- 40 mph.
- 50 mph.
- 60 mph.

A 30 mph limit usually applies where there are street lights but no speed limit signs.

1.19 On a three-lane dual carriageway the right-hand lane can be used for:
- overtaking only, never turning right.
- overtaking or turning right.
- fast-moving traffic only.
- turning right only, never overtaking.

You should normally use the left-hand lane on any dual carriageway unless you are overtaking or turning right. When overtaking on a dual carriageway, look for vehicles ahead that are turning right. They're likely to be slowing or stopped. You need to see them in good time so that you can take appropriate action.

1.20 You are approaching a busy junction. There are several lanes with road markings. At the last moment you realize that you are in the wrong lane. You should:

– continue in that lane.
– force your way across.
– stop until the area has cleared.
– use clear arm signals to cut across.

There are times where road markings can be obscured by queuing traffic, or you might be unsure which lane you need to be in.

If you realize that you're in the wrong lane, don't cut across lanes or bully other drivers to let you in. Follow the lane you're in and find somewhere safe to turn around if you need to.

1.21 You are joining a motorway. Why is it important to make full use of the slip road?

– because there is space available to turn round if you need to.
– to allow you direct access to the overtaking lanes.
– to build up a speed similar to traffic on the motorway.
– because you can continue on the hard shoulder.

Try to join the motorway without affecting the progress of the traffic already travelling on it. Always give way to traffic already on the motorway. At busy times you may have to slow down to merge into slow-moving traffic.

1.22 You keep well back while waiting to overtake a large vehicle. A car fills the gap. You should:

– sound your horn.
– drop back further.
– flash your headlights.
– start to overtake.

It's very frustrating when your separation distance is shortened by another vehicle. React positively, stay calm and drop further back.

1.23 You should always reduce your speed when travelling in fog because:

– the brakes do not work as well.
– you could be dazzled by other people's foglights.
– the engine is colder.
– it is more difficult to see events ahead.

You won't be able to see as far ahead in fog as you can on a clear day. You will need to reduce your speed so that, if a hazard looms out of the fog, you have the time and space to take avoiding action. Travelling in fog is hazardous. If you can, try and delay your journey until it has cleared.

1.24 You are on a narrow road at night. A slower-moving vehicle ahead has been signalling right for some time. What should you do?

- overtake on the left.
- flash your headlights before overtaking.
- signal right and sound your horn.
- wait for the signal to be cancelled before overtaking.

If the vehicle in front has been indicating right for some time, but has made no attempt to turn, wait for the signal to be cancelled. The other driver may have misjudged the distance to the road junction or there might be a hidden hazard.

1.25 You are on a country road. What should you expect to see coming towards you on *your* side of the road?

- motorcycles.
- bicycles.
- pedestrians.
- horse riders.

On a quiet country road always be aware that there may be a hazard just around the next bend, such as a slow-moving vehicle or pedestrians. Pedestrians are advised to walk on the right-hand side of the road if there is no pavement, so they may be walking towards you on your side of the road.

1.26 You are intending to turn right at a crossroads. An oncoming driver is also turning right. It will normally be safer to:

- keep the other vehicle to your right and turn behind it (offside to offside).
- keep the other vehicle to your left and turn in front of it (nearside to nearside).
- carry on and turn at the next junction instead.
- hold back and wait for the other driver to turn first.

At some junctions the layout may make it difficult to turn offside to offside. If this is the case, be prepared to pass nearside to nearside, but take extra care as your view ahead will be obscured by the vehicle turning in front of you.

1.27 You are signalling to turn right in busy traffic. How would you confirm your intention safely?

- sound the horn.
- give an arm signal.
- flash your headlights.
- position over the centre line.

In some situations you may feel your indicators cannot be seen by other road users. If you think you need to make your intention more clearly seen, give the arm signal shown in The Highway Code.

1.28 You are following a cyclist. You wish to turn left just ahead. You should:

- overtake the cyclist before the junction.
- pull alongside the cyclist and stay level until after the junction.
- hold back until the cyclist has passed the junction.
- go around the cyclist on the junction.

Make allowances for cyclists. Allow them plenty of room. Don't try to overtake and then turn left as you would have to cut in across the path of the cyclist. Be patient and stay behind them until they have passed the junction.

1.29 You are following a car driven by an elderly driver. You should:

- expect the driver to drive badly.
- flash your lights and overtake.
- be aware that the driver's reactions may not be as fast as yours.
- stay very close behind but be careful.

You must show consideration to other road users. The reactions of elderly drivers may be slower and they might need more time to deal with a situation. Be tolerant and don't lose patience or show your annoyance.

1.30 You are turning left into a side road. Pedestrians are crossing the road near the junction. You must:

- wave them on.
- sound your horn.
- switch on your hazard lights.
- wait for them to cross.

Check that it's clear before you turn into a junction. If there are pedestrians crossing, let them cross in their own time.

1.31 For which of these situations should you use hazard warning lights?
- stopping on double yellow lines.
- temporarily obstructing traffic.
- parking on the pavement.
- parking in a restricted area.

Hazard warning lights are an important safety feature. Use them when driving on a motorway to warn traffic behind you of danger ahead. You should also use them if your vehicle has broken down and is causing an obstruction.

1.32 Another vehicle is taking a long time to overtake you. Which of the following should you do?
- increase your speed to leave them behind.
- be prepared to slow down and let them pass.
- brake hard and let them pass.
- flash your headlights to warn oncoming traffic.

Overtaking is one of the major causes of serious collisions. Never accelerate when someone is overtaking you. Be prepared to ease off, if necessary, to help them pass you. A good driver should recognize how vulnerable the overtaking vehicle could be if confronted by any vehicle approaching in the opposite direction.

1.33 When approaching a left-hand bend, you should position your vehicle:
- where you get the best view.
- towards the centre of the road.
- towards the right of your lane.
- in the centre of your lane.

Keep to the centre of your lane as you approach. Don't move to the centre of the road to improve your view. This could put you too close to oncoming traffic and a vehicle coming the other way might be taking the bend wide.

1.34 You intend to turn left at traffic lights. Just before turning you should:
- check your right hand mirror.
- move closer to the vehicle in front.
- straddle the lanes.
- check for cycles on your left.

Check your nearside for cyclists before moving away. This is especially important if you have been in a stationary queue of traffic and are about to move off, as cyclists often try to filter past on the nearside of stationary vehicles.

1.35 You need to reverse park between two vehicles. As a guideline the minimum gap between the two vehicles should be:

- one and a half times the length of your car.
- one and a half times the length of the object car.
- two times the length of your car.
- two times the length of the object car.

When you have mastered the techniques ,you should be able to park between two vehicles in a gap that would normally be about one and a half times the length of your own vehicle.

1.36 You are turning right at a mini-roundabout which has central markings. You will normally:

- drive around them.
- take the shortest route.
- drive over them.
- take the most direct route.

You should approach mini-roundabouts in the same way as normal roundabouts. All vehicles must pass round the central markings except large vehicles or vehicles towing a trailer, which are physically incapable of doing so.

1.37 When driving in traffic lanes a driver should drive:

- well to the left of the lane.
- well to the right of the lane.
- in the centre of the lane.
- anywhere within the lane.

You should always follow lane markings, which are there for two reasons: they make the best possible use of road space; and they guide the traffic. Keeping within your lane is important.

1.38 The centre lane of a three-lane motorway is for:

- overtaking slower moving vehicles on your left.
- overtaking vehicles on your right.
- when travelling at a constant speed of 60 mph or less.
- maintaining a speed of between 60 mph and 70 mph.

Keep to the left-hand lane unless there are a great many slower vehicles ahead. Avoid repeatedly changing lane; it may be safer to remain in the centre lane until the manoeuvre is completed.

1.39 When driving on a three-lane motorway you may:

- always overtake on the left if you are within one mile of your exit.
- not overtake on the left at any time.
- overtake on the left if traffic on the right of you is in a queue moving more slowly than you are.
- overtake stationary traffic by driving along the hard shoulder.

Stay in your lane if traffic is moving slowly in queues. If the queue on your right is moving more slowly than you are, you may pass on the left.

1.40 You are crossing a dual carriageway from a side road. The central reservation is too narrow for the length of your vehicle. You should:

- move to the central reservation close to the other carriageway and go when a safe gap occurs.
- wait in the side road, until you can cross the dual carriageway in one movement.
- wait for a gap in the traffic then move forward blocking the first half of the road and proceed when safe.
- wait in the side road until someone gives way.

If the central reservation can't contain the length of your vehicle, you must not begin to cross until the dual carriageway is clear in both directions. Don't emerge unless you're sure you won't cause traffic to alter speed or course. This is particularly important if you're driving a longer vehicle or towing a caravan or trailer.

Band 2 – Traffic signs and signals, car control, pedestrians, mechanical knowledge

2.1 When you approach a bus signalling to move off from a bus stop you should:

- get past before it moves.
- allow it to pull away, if it is safe to do so.
- flash your headlights as you approach.
- signal left and wave the bus on.

Give way to buses if you can do so safely, especially when they signal to pull away from bus stops. Look out for people who've just got off the bus as they may try to cross the road. Don't try to accelerate past before the bus moves away and don't flash your lights; other road users may be misled by this.

2.2   Which of these vehicles is *least* likely to be affected by crosswinds?
- cyclists.
- motorcyclists.
- high-sided vehicles.
- cars.

Although cars are the least likely to be affected, crosswinds can take anyone by surprise, especially:

- *after overtaking a large vehicle;*
- *when passing gaps between hedges or buildings;*
- *on exposed sections of road.*

2.3   What is the national speed limit for cars on motorways?
- 30 mph.
- 50 mph.
- 60 mph.
- 70 mph.

Travelling at the national speed limit doesn't allow you to stay in the right-hand lane. Always use the left-hand lane whenever possible. When leaving the motorway, always adjust your speed in good time to deal with bends or curves on the slip road or traffic queuing at roundabouts.

2.4   You are driving on a motorway. There are red flashing lights above every lane. You must:
- pull onto the hard shoulder.
- slow down and watch for further signals.
- leave at the next exit.
- stop and wait.

Red flashing lights above every lane mean you must not go on any further. You'll also see a red cross illuminated. Stop and wait. Don't:

- *change lanes;*
- *continue;*
- *pull onto the hard shoulder (unless in an emergency).*

2.5   On a motorway the amber reflective studs can be found between:
- the hard shoulder and the carriageway.
- the acceleration lane and the carriageway.
- the central reservation and the carriageway.
- each pair of the lanes.

On motorways reflective studs are fitted into the road to help you:
- *in the dark;*
- *in conditions of poor visibility.*

Amber-coloured studs are on the right-hand edge of the main carriageway, next to the central reservation.

2.6   What colour are the reflective studs between the lanes on a motorway?
- green.
- amber.
- white.
- red.

White studs are put between the lanes on motorways. The light from your headlights is reflected back and this is especially useful in bad weather, when visibility is restricted.

2.7   What colour are the reflective studs between a motorway and its slip road?
- amber.
- white.
- green.
- red.

The studs between the carriageway and the hard shoulder are normally red. These change to green where there is a slip road. They will help you identify slip roads when visibility is poor or when it is dark.

2.8   What is the national speed limit on a single-carriageway road for cars and motorcycles?
- 30 mph.
- 50 mph.
- 60 mph.
- 70 mph.

Exceeding the speed limit is dangerous and can result in you receiving penalty points on your licence. It isn't worth it. You should know the speed limit for the road that you're on by observing the road signs. Different speed limits apply if you are towing a trailer.

2.9 What is the national speed limit for cars and motorcycles on a dual carriageway?

- 30 mph.
- 50 mph.
- 60 mph.
- 70 mph.

Ensure that you know the speed limit for the road that you're on. The speed limit on a dual carriageway or motorway is 70 mph for cars and motorcycles, unless there are signs to indicate otherwise. The speed limits for different types of vehicles are listed in The Highway Code.

2.10 You may wait in a yellow box junction when you are:

- prevented from turning right, only by oncoming traffic.
- in a queue of traffic turning left.
- in a queue of traffic to go ahead.
- on a roundabout.

The purpose of this road marking is to keep the junction clear of queuing traffic. You may only wait in the marked area when you're turning right and your exit lane is clear but you can't complete the turn because of oncoming traffic.

2.11 You may only enter a yellow box junction when:

- there are fewer than two vehicles in front of you.
- the traffic lights show green.
- your exit road is clear.
- you need to turn left.

Box junctions are marked on the road to prevent the road becoming blocked. Don't enter the box unless your exit road is clear. You may only wait in the box if your exit road is clear but oncoming traffic is preventing you from completing the turn.

2.12 At a pelican crossing the flashing amber light means you:

- must not move off until the lights stop flashing.
- must give way to pedestrians still on the crossing.
- can move off, even if pedestrians are still on the crossing.
- must stop because the lights are about to change to red.

If there is no one on the crossing when the amber light is flashing, you may proceed over the crossing. You don't need to wait for the green light to show.

2.13 White markers with red stripes indicate that you are approaching:

- the end of a motorway.
- a concealed level crossing.
- a concealed speed limit sign.
- the end of a dual carriageway.

If there is a bend just before the level crossing you may not be able to see the level crossing barriers or waiting traffic. These signs give you an early warning that you may find these hazards just around the bend.

2.14 At toucan crossings, apart from pedestrians you should be aware of:

- emergency vehicles emerging.
- buses pulling out.
- trams crossing in front.
- cyclists riding across.

Pedestrians and cyclists will see the green signal together. Cyclists are permitted to ride across.

2.15 Which shape is used for a GIVE WAY sign?

- square.
- circular.
- octagonal.
- triangular.

Other warning signs are the same shape and colour, but the GIVE WAY sign is the only triangular one that points downwards. When you see this sign you must give way to traffic on the road which you are about to enter.

2.16 At a junction you see an octagonal sign but it is partly covered by snow. What does it mean?

- Crossroads.
- Give way.
- Stop.
- Turn right.

The STOP sign is the only road sign that is octagonal. This is so that it can be recognized and obeyed even if it is obscured, for example by snow.

2.17 You *must* obey signs giving orders. These signs are mostly in:

- green rectangles.
- red triangles.
- blue rectangles.
- red circles.

Traffic signs can be divided into three classes. Those giving orders, those warning and those informing. Warning signs are usually triangular and direction signs are generally rectangular. One notable exception is the octagonal STOP sign.

2.18 What shape is a STOP sign at a junction?

- circular.
- triangular.
- rectangular.
- octagonal.

To make it easy to recognize, the STOP sign is the only sign of this shape. You must stop and make effective observation before proceeding.

2.19 At traffic lights, amber on its own means:

- prepare to go.
- go if the way is clear.
- go if no pedestrians are crossing.
- stop at the stop line.

As you approach traffic lights that have been on green for some time, anticipate that they will soon change to amber and then red. Be ready for this so that you are able to stop in time.

2.20 A red traffic light means:

- you should stop unless turning left.
- stop, if you are able to brake safely.
- you must stop and wait behind the stop line.
- proceed with caution.

Traffic lights change in a set cycle. By learning the sequence you will know what light is coming on next when approaching junctions. This will help you to plan and adjust your speed accordingly.

2.21 Triangular signs are to give:
- warnings.
- information.
- orders.
- directions.

This type of sign will warn you of hazards ahead. Make sure you look at each sign that you pass on the road, so that you do not miss any vital instructions or information.

2.22 You are approaching a red traffic light. The signal will change from red to:
- red and amber, then green.
- green, then amber.
- amber, then green.
- green and amber, then green.

If you know which light is going to show next you can plan your approach accordingly. This can help prevent excessive braking or hesitation at the junction.

2.23 Tyre pressures should be checked:
- every time the car is driven.
- at least once a week.
- at least once a month.
- only when the tyres look soft.

Check all tyres (including the spare) at least once a week. Do it when they are cold and remember to refit the valve caps. The handbook will tell you if you need different pressures for different conditions. Remember, it's so dangerous that it's an offence to use a vehicle with a tyre not properly inflated.

2.24 The level of the fluid in the brake fluid reservoir falls too low. This could result in:
- complete loss of braking on the footbrake.
- serious brake fade on hills.
- some loss of braking on the handbrake.
- complete loss of braking on the handbrake.

Driving a vehicle with a brake defect could be dangerous and may constitute an offence. Check the brake fluid level regularly by using the high/low markers on the reservoir. If the fluid level is too low it could result in loss of braking efficiency.

2.25 At puffin crossings, which light will not show to a driver?
- flashing amber.
- red.
- steady amber.
- green.

A flashing amber light is shown at pelican crossings, but puffin crossings are different. They are controlled electronically and automatically detect when pedestrians are on the crossing. The phase is shortened or lengthened according to the position of the pedestrians.

2.26 You should use hazard warning lights when:
- you are double parked on a two-way road.
- your direction indicators are not working.
- warning oncoming traffic that you intend to stop.
- your vehicle has broken down and is causing an obstruction.

Hazard lights will warn other traffic that there is a potential hazard ahead. If you repair your vehicle don't forget to turn them off again when you move away.

2.27 You should make sure that your indicators are cancelled after turning to avoid:
- flattening the battery.
- misleading other road users.
- dazzling other road users.
- damage to the indicator relay.

If you haven't taken a sharp turn your indicators might not turn off automatically. Be aware of this if you've used them for slight deviations, such as passing parked vehicles.

2.28 You may use hazard warning lights when:
- driving on a motorway to warn traffic behind of a hazard ahead.
- you are double parked on a two-way road.
- your direction indicators are not working.
- warning oncoming traffic that you intend to stop.

Hazard warning lights may be used when slowing suddenly on a motorway or unrestricted dual carriageway to warn the traffic behind. Never use hazard warning lights to excuse dangerous or illegal parking.

2.29 The main cause of brake fade is:
- – the brakes overheating.
- – air in the brake fluid.
- – oil on the brakes.
- – the brakes are out of adjustment.

If your vehicle is fitted with drum brakes they can get hot and lose efficiency. This happens when they're used continually, such as on a long, steep, downhill stretch of road. Using a lower gear will assist the braking and help prevent the vehicle gaining momentum.

2.30 What can cause heavy steering?
- – driving on ice.
- – badly worn brakes.
- – over-inflated tyres.
- – under-inflated tyres.

If your tyres don't have enough air in them they'll drag against the surface of the road and this makes the steering feel heavy. As well as steering, under-inflated tyres can affect:

- ● *braking;*
- ● *cornering;*
- ● *fuel consumption.*

It is an offence to drive with tyres that are not properly inflated.

2.31 A bus lane on your left shows no times of operation. This means it is:
- – not in operation at all.
- – only in operation at peak times.
- – in operation 24 hours a day.
- – only in operation in daylight hours.

Don't drive or park in a bus lane when it's in operation. This can cause disruption to traffic and delays to public transport.

2.32 New petrol-engined cars must be fitted with catalytic converters. The reason for this is to:
- – control exhaust noise levels.
- – prolong the life of the exhaust system.
- – allow the exhaust system to be recycled.
- – reduce harmful exhaust emissions.

We should all be concerned about the effect traffic has on our environment. Fumes from vehicles are polluting the air around us. Catalytic converters act like a filter, removing some of the toxic waste from exhaust gases.

2.33 A roof rack fitted to your car will:

- reduce fuel consumption.
- improve the road handling.
- make your car go faster.
- increase fuel consumption.

If you are carrying anything on a roof rack, make sure that any cover is securely fitted and does not flap about while driving. Aerodynamically designed roof boxes are available which reduce wind resistance and in turn fuel consumption.

2.34 You are driving down a steep hill. Why could keeping the clutch down or selecting neutral for too long be dangerous?

- fuel consumption will be higher.
- your vehicle will pick up speed.
- it will damage the engine.
- it will wear tyres out more quickly.

Driving in neutral or with the clutch down for long periods is known as 'coasting'. There will be no engine braking and your vehicle will pick up speed on downhill slopes. Coasting can be very dangerous because it reduces steering and braking control.

2.35 You are driving down a long steep hill. You suddenly notice your brakes are not working as well as normal. What is the usual cause of this?

- the brakes overheating.
- air in the brake fluid.
- oil on the brakes.
- badly adjusted brakes.

This is more likely to happen on vehicles fitted with drum brakes but can still apply to disc brakes as well. Using a lower gear will assist the braking and help you to keep control of your vehicle.

2.36 Pressing the clutch pedal down or rolling in neutral for too long while driving will:

- use more fuel.
- cause the engine to overheat.
- reduce your control.
- improve tyre wear.

Holding the clutch down or staying in neutral for too long will cause your vehicle to freewheel. This is known as 'coasting' and it is dangerous as it reduces your control of the vehicle.

2.37 You are in the right-hand lane of a dual carriageway. You see signs showing that the right lane is closed 800 yards ahead. You should:
- keep in that lane until you reach the queue.
- move to the left immediately.
- wait and see which lane is moving faster.
- move to the left in good time.

Lane closures are normally found near roadworks. Use your mirrors and move into the correct lane for your vehicle in good time. Look out for additional signs and comply with them.

2.38 Which of the following will improve fuel consumption?
- short journeys with a cold engine.
- planning well ahead.
- late and harsh braking.
- driving in lower gears.

Plan your journey beforehand and try to use non-congested routes. Repeated stopping and starting in queues and travelling in low gears for long distances will use a lot more fuel than keeping up a steady pace.

2.39 Why could keeping the clutch down or selecting neutral for long periods of time be dangerous?
- fuel spillage will occur.
- engine damage may be caused.
- you will have less steering and braking control.
- it will wear tyres out more quickly.

Letting your vehicle roll or coast in neutral reduces your control over steering and braking. This can be dangerous on downhill slopes where your vehicle could pick up speed very quickly.

2.40 You are approaching a zebra crossing and pedestrians are waiting to cross. You should:
- give way to the elderly and infirm only.
- slow down and prepare to stop.
- use your headlights to indicate they can cross.
- wave at them to cross the road.

When approaching a zebra crossing a driver should look out for pedestrians that may intend to use it to cross the road. A pupil must be taught to give way and stop if necessary when someone has stepped onto the path of the crossing.

Band 3 – Driving test, disabilities, law

3.1 What is the nearest you may park to a junction?
- 10 metres (32 feet).
- 12 metres (39 feet).
- 15 metres (49 feet).
- 20 metres (66 feet).

Don't park within 10 metres (32 feet) of a junction (unless in an authorized parking place). This is to allow drivers emerging from, or turning into, the junction a clear view of the road they are joining. It also allows them to see hazards such as pedestrians or cyclists at the junction.

3.2 You must not use your horn when you are stationary:
- unless a moving vehicle may cause you danger.
- at any time whatsoever.
- unless it is used only briefly.
- except for signalling that you have just arrived.

Only sound you horn when stationary if you think there is a risk of danger. Do not use it to attract attention. This causes unnecessary noise and could be misleading to other road users.

3.3 A driving test pass certificate is valid for a maximum period of:
- one year.
- two years.
- three years.
- 10 years.

After a person passes the test their full licence is normally issued directly from the licensing authority (DVLA or DVA NI). However, if this doesn't happen they should apply for a full licence as soon as possible. The certificate is valid for two years; if they don't apply within that time they will need to retake their test.

3.4 During the driving test a candidate coasts up to and around corners. The marking on the driving test report will be: 'Control …
- gears.'
- gears and clutch.'
- clutch.'
- footbrake and clutch.'

You should not coast with the clutch pedal depressed or the gear lever in neutral. It reduces the driver's control of the vehicle.

3.5 When carrying out the emergency stop exercise during a driving test a candidate will be expected:

- to use the mirrors before braking.
- not to use the mirrors.
- to use the mirrors while braking.
- to use all the mirrors then brake.

A good driver should be checking the mirrors frequently to suit the prevailing road and traffic conditions and be aware of what is happening all around. Additionally, the examiner will ensure that there is no potential danger before asking the candidate to carry out the exercise.

3.6 A car is fitted with a dual accelerator, clutch and brake pedals. On a driving test, which of the pedals must be removed?

- clutch and brake.
- accelerator and clutch.
- clutch.
- accelerator.

While dual accelerators are not normally fitted to training vehicles, if one is fitted, it must be removed while the vehicle is being used for a driving test. This is for safety reasons.

3.7 It is a driver's responsibility to ensure that the front-seat passenger wears a seat belt if the passenger is under:

- 14 years old.
- 15 years old.
- 16 years old.
- 18 years old.

Seat belts save lives and reduce the risk of injury. It's your legal responsibility to ensure that all passengers under 14 years old wear a seat belt, or are fastened in an approved child restraint. However, it's good practice to ensure that all other passengers wear seat belts.

3.8 When learning to drive, pupils must be accompanied by a person who has held a full driving licence for the category of vehicle being driven for at least:

- three years and who is at least 21 years of age.
- three years and who is at least 25 years of age.
- four years and who is at least 21 years of age.
- four years and who is at least 25 years of age.

Anyone who accompanies a learner car driver must have held, and still hold, a full EC/EEA licence (in that category) for at least three years and be at least 21 years old. This still applies even if they are just helping a friend and no money is exchanged.

3.9 Drivers convicted of certain dangerous driving offences are required to take an extended driving test, which:

- is the same length of time as the ordinary L test.
- takes about 70 minutes and will include additional manoeuvres.
- takes about 70 minutes and will include the same manoeuvres as the ordinary L test.
- is concentrated on their conviction.

The extended test takes about 70 minutes and is assessed to the same standard as the ordinary L test.

3.10 An instructor whose name has been entered on the Register of Approved Driving Instructors will be subject to supervision by a Supervising Examiner (ADI):

- only for the first six months that they are on the Register.
- for the whole time that they are on the Register.
- only for the first 12 months that they are on the Register.
- only until they achieve a grade 6.

As part of the regulations, you must undergo a periodic test of continued ability and fitness to give instruction. The check test should be approached with a positive attitude. It is also the opportunity for the ADI to raise any other issues.

3.11 During the driving test your pupil is carrying out the 'left reverse' exercise. After entering the side road, they should:

- continue to reverse for some distance, keeping reasonably close to the kerb.
- continue to drive in reverse gear until asked to stop by the examiner.
- reverse just far enough to allow them to pull out and go in the opposite direction.
- continue to reverse for some distance, keeping well away from the kerb.

Reverse for a reasonable distance to clear the mouth of the junction and pull up in a safe position.

3.12 A candidate on a driving test can be accompanied by:

- anyone aged 16 or over.
- only a driving instructor.
- no other person.
- only an interpreter.

Anyone can accompany a candidate on an L driving test with the candidate's agreement. At the start of the test the examiner will ask them if they wish their ADI or accompanying driver to be present on test. They must be 16 years or older and wear a seat belt whilst in the vehicle. They cannot take any part in the test.

3.13 The item 'Use of speed' is marked on the driving test report. This means that the candidate was:

- driving too fast for the road and traffic conditions.
- approaching junctions too fast.
- driving too slowly for the road and traffic conditions.
- approaching junctions too slowly.

A driver should make safe, reasonable progress along the road bearing in mind the speed limit, road, traffic and weather conditions. A pupil needs to understand and demonstrate competence in making progress but should neither drive too fast for the prevailing situation nor change their speed unpredictably.

3.14 An examiner gives the signal for an emergency stop. A candidate should react by:

- braking promptly.
- checking the mirrors.
- depressing the clutch.
- steering to the left.

In an emergency a pupil should be trained to stop the vehicle as quickly and as safely as possible. Full control should be maintained. The examiner will check that the road is clear behind before the signal to stop is given.

3.15 A category B driving test candidate with sight in only one eye passes the test. The examiner will issue a:

- pass certificate showing the disability.
- normal pass certificate.
- pass certificate, with a restriction listing the vehicles which the person can drive.
- pass certificate restricting the person to certain speed limits.

A successful candidate with vision in only one eye will be issued with a normal certificate. As with all drivers, the licensing authority must be notified of any medical conditions when applying for a licence and when they develop or change.

3.16 Learner drivers in a car must be supervised by someone who is:

- 18 (or over) and who has held a full licence for that category of vehicle for one year.
- 20 (or over) and has held a full licence for that category for three years.
- 21 (or over) and who has held a full licence for that category of vehicle for at least three years.
- 21 (or over) and who has held a full licence for that category of vehicle for at least one year.

A person who accompanies a learner must have held a full EC/EEA driving licence for at least three years and still hold one for the category of vehicle being used by the learner driver. The accompanying driver must be at least 21 years of age. All Approved Driving Instructors meet that criterion and many more.

3.17 Unless road signs indicate otherwise, the speed limit on a two-way road outside a built-up area is:

- 30 mph.
- 50 mph.
- 60 mph.
- 70 mph.

You don't have to drive up to the speed limit. Use your own judgement and drive at a speed that suits the prevailing road, weather and traffic conditions while keeping within the speed limit.

3.18 A vehicle fitted with a dual accelerator is to be used for a driving test. This pedal or lever must be:

- disconnected.
- blanked off.
- removed.
- in working order.

It is a requirement of the driving test that if a dual accelerator is fitted to a vehicle, it must be removed before the test.

3.19 A pupil who is colour-blind:

- must have a doctor's certificate allowing them to drive.
- is allowed to drive without restriction.
- is not legally allowed to drive.
- must have glasses with special lenses.

A person who is colour-blind will have to pass the same eyesight test as any other candidate on a driving test.

3.20 On the driving test report your candidate has a serious mark for 'Use of mirrors –signalling'. This means that the:
- candidate didn't use the mirrors effectively and act accordingly.
- candidate's attention was directed towards the front and rear of their car equally.
- mirrors were not clean and adjusted correctly.
- candidate didn't check the blind spot before signalling.

Each stage of the MSM routine should always be considered and applied as appropriate when approaching a hazard or carrying out a manoeuvre. Looking in the mirror is not sufficient. It is important that a driver is trained to make effective use of the mirrors and act accordingly on what was seen in them. Failing to do so can have serious consequences.

3.21 The wearing of a seat belt by a 16-year-old front-seat passenger is the responsibility of the:
- driver.
- front-seat passenger.
- parent/guardian.
- owner of the car.

Passengers over the age of 14 are responsible to ensure that they wear a seat belt when it is fitted in a vehicle. It must be worn unless that person is exempt. However, a responsible driver will ensure that all passengers wear seat belts.

3.22 Where an MOT certificate has expired, you:
- may continue using the vehicle providing it passes the MOT test within one calendar month.
- may drive to and from an MOT test appointment.
- must arrange for the MOT testing station to collect the car on a trailer.
- should inform your insurance company.

Cars and motorcycles must normally pass an MOT test three years from the date of the first registration and every year after that. The vehicle must not be driven without an MOT certificate when it should have one. Exceptionally, the vehicle may be driven to a pre-arranged test appointment or to a garage for repairs required for the test.

3.23 You must not drive if your breath alcohol level is higher than:
- 20 microgrammes per 100 millilitres.
- 25 microgrammes per 100 millilitres.
- 30 microgrammes per 100 millilitres.
- 35 microgrammes per 100 millilitres.

Do not drink and drive as it will seriously affect your judgement and abilities. Alcohol will give a false sense of confidence, will reduce coordination and slow down reactions. It will take time to leave your body. If you are going to drink, arrange another means of transport.

3.24 Car passengers *must* wear a seat belt if one is available, unless they are:
- under 14 years old.
- under 1.5 metres (5 feet) in height.
- sitting in the rear seat.
- exempt for medical reasons.

If you have adult passengers it is their responsibility to wear a seat belt, but you should still remind them to put them on as they get in the car.

3.25 Before driving anyone else's motor vehicle you should make sure that:
- the vehicle owner has third-party insurance cover.
- your own vehicle has insurance cover.
- the vehicle is insured for your use.
- the owner has left the insurance documents in the vehicle.

Driving a vehicle without insurance cover is illegal. If you cause injury to anyone or damage to property it could be very expensive and you could also be subject to a criminal prosecution. You can arrange insurance cover with:

- *an insurance company;*
- *a broker;*
- *some motor manufacturers or dealers.*

3.26 You are towing a trailer with your car on a motorway. What is your maximum speed limit?
- 40 mph.
- 50 mph.
- 60 mph.
- 70 mph.

Don't forget that you're towing a trailer. If you're towing a small, light trailer it won't reduce your vehicle's performance by very much. However, strong winds or buffeting from large vehicles might cause the trailer to snake from side to side. Be aware of your speed and don't exceed the lower limit imposed.

3.27 As a car driver which of these lanes are you *not* normally allowed to use?
- crawler lane.
- cycle lane.
- overtaking lane.
- acceleration lane.

A driver must not park or drive in a cycle lane marked by a solid white line during its times of operation. The exception may be where the cycle lane is marked by a broken white line and it is unavoidable to do so.

3.28 The legal minimum depth of tread for car tyres over three-quarters of the breadth is:
- 1.0 mm.
- 1.6 mm.
- 2.5 mm.
- 4.0 mm.

Tyres must have sufficient depth of tread to give them a good grip on the road surface. The legal minimum for cars is 1.6 mm. This depth should be across the central three-quarters of the breadth of the tyre and around the entire circumference.

3.29 It is illegal to drive with tyres that:
- have been bought second-hand.
- have a large deep cut in the side wall.
- are of different makes.
- are of different tread patterns.

When checking your tyres for cuts and bulges in the side walls don't forget the inner walls (ie those facing each other under the vehicle).

3.30 Your car needs an MOT certificate. If you drive without one this could invalidate your:
- vehicle service record.
- insurance.
- road tax disc.
- vehicle registration document.

If your vehicle requires an MOT certificate, it is illegal to drive it without one that is valid. As well as it being illegal, the vehicle may also be unsafe for use on the road and could endanger you, any passengers and other road users. Without a valid MOT certificate your insurance is invalid.

3.31 When is it legal to drive a car over three years old without an MOT certificate?

- up to seven days after the old certificate has run out.
- when driving to an MOT centre to arrange an appointment.
- just after buying a second hand car with no MOT.
- when driving to an appointment at an MOT centre.

Any car over three years old must have a valid MOT certificate before it can be used on the road. The only time a car is exempt is when it's being driven to an appointment at an MOT testing station.

3.32 Front fog lights must *only* be used when:

- your headlights are not working.
- they are operated with rear fog lights.
- they were fitted by the vehicle manufacturer.
- visibility is seriously reduced.

Fog lights will help others see you, but remember, they must only be used if visibility is seriously reduced to less than 100 metres (328 feet).

3.33 Front fog lights may be used *only* if:

- visibility is seriously reduced.
- they are fitted above the bumper.
- they are not as bright as the headlights.
- an audible warning device is used.

Your vehicle should have a warning light on the dashboard which illuminates when the fog lights are being used. You need to be familiar with the layout of your dashboard so you are aware if they have been switched on in error, or you have forgotten to switch them off.

3.34 You may cross double white lines along the centre of the road to overtake if you:

- are passing traffic that is queuing back at a junction with a major road.
- can clearly see that there are no obstructions on the right-hand side of the road.
- are passing a road maintenance vehicle that is travelling at less than 10 mph.
- are passing a car that is slowing down to turn left into a minor road.

Generally you must not cross or straddle solid white lines along the centre of the road. There some exceptions and these include when you need to enter premises or a side road, to pass a stationary vehicle, pedal cycle, horse or road maintenance vehicle when they are travelling at 10 mph or less. In addition you must not park on such a road except to pick up or set down passengers.

3.35 You are on a road that has no speed limit repeater signs. There are street lights. What is the speed limit?

- 30 mph.
- 40 mph.
- 50 mph.
- 60 mph.

If you aren't sure of the speed limit a good indication is the presence of street lights. If there is street lighting the speed limit will usually be 30 mph unless otherwise indicated.

3.36 What rules apply to a driving school car that is being used in a driving test?

- it can be fitted with dual controls including a dual accelerator that is operable.
- it can be fitted with dual controls provided no dual accelerator is fitted.
- it must be fitted with a dual brake and dual clutch.
- it must be fitted with a dual brake, clutch and accelerator.

For safety reasons any dual accelerator must be removed before a vehicle is used by a candidate on a driving test.

3.37 You are instructing a pupil about turning the vehicle around. When may you remove your seat belt?

- only when asked to do so by the pupil.
- during any manoeuvre that involves reversing.
- if the pupil holds an 'Exemption Certificate'.
- only when the vehicle is actually reversing.

Drivers and passengers must wear seat belts. There are a few exemptions. If necessary a driver may remove their seat belt when carrying out an exercise that involves reversing. This also applies to instructors while supervising such manoeuvres. Realistically, with modern inertia-reel belts it's not usually necessary to remove them.

3.38 When driving, a newly qualified driver must:

- display green L plates.
- not exceed 40 mph for 12 months.
- be accompanied on a motorway.
- have valid motor insurance.

As an ADI you should advise your pupil that it is their responsibility to make sure the vehicle they intend to drive is properly insured and meets all other legal requirements.

3.39 During a driving test when an examiner is assessing the candidate's driving ability, they will record:

- all the faults made by the candidate.
- no more than four driving faults in any one assessment box.
- a limited number of faults in order to avoid embarrassing the candidate.
- only those faults that are of sufficient significance.

All examiners are trained to assess and mark driving tests to a common standard set by the Driving Standards Agency. An error committed by a test candidate that is worthy of being recorded will be marked on the driving test report. Pupils should be advised that, while there is no such person as the perfect driver, they should try not to worry about any fault they think they may have made. The fault may not be significant enough to be recorded, or assessed as serious.

3.40 A driver (not subject to the New Drivers Act) will be disqualified if they accumulate 12 or more penalty points within a *maximum* period of:

- six months.
- three years.
- four years.
- five years.

All drivers should consider 'safe driving for life'. If they do accumulate 12 or more penalty points within a three-year period, they will be disqualified. This will be for a minimum period of six months, or longer, if the driver has previously been disqualified. They may have to start again as a provisional driver.

Band 4 – Publications, instructional techniques

4.1 Using demonstration as a teaching method is usually followed by:

- consolidation of the skill by means of practice.
- detailed analysis of the manoeuvre carried out.
- discussion with the pupil of possible faults which may occur.
- the introduction of a new subject.

Demonstration, where appropriate, is a valuable tool in the instructional process. Having verbally explained and then given a demonstration on a particular aspect the instructor should plan to allow practical development at the earliest opportunity.

4.2   You are teaching the turn in the road manoeuvre. Your pupil is reversing across the road. They should look:

- over the left shoulder only.
- over the right shoulder only.
- effectively over both shoulders.
- continually in the mirrors.

All-round observation is essential throughout the manoeuvre and in particular when reversing across the carriageway. Look out for pedestrians as well as other road users while completing the exercise.

4.3   A pupil drives the rear wheels over the kerb when turning left. They should be told that:

- this fault can be avoided by swinging out to the right after turning.
- the rear wheels cut in when turning left.
- this fault can be avoided by swinging out to the right before turning.
- they had turned the steering wheel too late.

An instructor should clearly analyse a fault and get to the main cause of the problem. Having given appropriate feedback, further practice should be given to remedy the problem.

4.4   The 'gestalt' method of learning is based on:

- understanding of subject matter.
- repeatedly practising a skill.
- reflex actions.
- muscle memory.

People's perception of situations can vary as they see things in different ways. The instructor's difficulty is to concentrate the pupil's attention on the subject matter. In order to achieve this the instructor needs to ensure that the lesson content is interesting.

4.5   When starting on a downhill gradient, pupils should be taught to use:

- the lowest available gear.
- the appropriate gear for the slope.
- the highest available gear.
- a lower gear than normal.

The routine is simpler than moving off uphill because the weight of the vehicle helps you to move away. Be careful to use the appropriate gear for the steepness of the slope.

4.6 If a pupil under instruction fails to make progress the instructor should:

- be patient and continue the well-tried methods which are working with other pupils.
- vary the methods of instruction being used.
- allow the pupil to go with another instructor.
- continue to repeat the exercise until the pupil gets it right.

If your usual techniques or methods do not appear to be working, discuss the matter with your pupil, and explore alternative ways of trying to get the point across.

4.7 The 'learning plateau' sometimes occurs during instruction. This refers to:

- a slowing down of the pace of instruction.
- a common difficulty experienced by some persons in hand–foot coordination.
- a temporary halt in the learning process.
- persons who have learning difficulties.

An instructor must be able to recognize when a pupil has reached the 'learning plateau' during a training session. In that situation it is a good idea to consolidate what has been covered to date. Pupils learn at different rates and some pass through this stage quicker than others.

4.8 When teaching a pupil who continually drives too fast, in all situations, you should:

- explain what can happen as a result of speed.
- impose a speed limit lower than everyone else's.
- let them learn from experience using the dual brake to ensure safety.
- give more demonstrations than normal.

Simply telling a pupil that they are driving too fast is not sufficient. Explanations need to be given of what may occur if they repeat the fault. More importantly they need to know what to do, to prevent it happening again.

4.9 Transfer of learning can often be of value when giving driving instruction. This process is where:

- parents take on the responsibility for teaching their children to drive.
- associations are made with previously acquired skills and knowledge.
- trainees learn from friends and colleagues.
- pupils learn from their mistakes.

An instructor should try and establish links between previous experience and the new skills to be acquired. For example, a pedestrian that can judge appropriate gaps in the traffic to cross the road can link this skill to turning right into side roads.

4.10 As a pupil's knowledge and driving competence increase, the level of instructor involvement is likely to:

- remain the same.
- increase.
- decrease.
- finish.

Detailed instruction should decrease as the pupil's level of ability increases. An instructor should not be controlling the pupil all of the time. This takes the initiative away from the pupil and could be considered as over-instruction.

4.11 A pupil can be encouraged to develop a good driving attitude by:

- persuasion and example.
- an instructor imposing their will.
- letting them learn from experience.
- asking them to study the instruction manuals.

A positive driving attitude should be instigated by the instructor. This can begin on the initial meeting and continue throughout a pupil's development. The instructor's attitude to actions and occurrences between the pupil and other road users should be professional at all times.

4.12 When teaching a pupil to drive a car in a smooth and coordinated manner the area of activity where learning will mainly take place will be:

- psychomotor.
- emotional.
- intellectual.
- psychological.

Psychomotor activities relate to practical skills. When driving a vehicle, a pupil will need to learn how to manipulate each control in a competent manner. The next stage will be to combine their use and coordinate actions smoothly to complete a task. In the early stages of learning an example would be to move away smoothly without stalling.

4.13 In choosing a method of instruction an instructor should:
- maintain a consistent approach to be fair to all pupils.
- vary the method to suit the individual pupil.
- use one of two distinct approaches.
- stick to the lesson plan.

A good instructor will have the ability to transfer information in a variety of different ways, so that the instruction offered will suit the individual needs of each pupil. It should be remembered that a majority of pupils may have different levels of ability. Training should be adjusted accordingly.

4.14 Persons suffering from a medical condition requiring treatment by drugs should initially, before driving, consult the:
- Vehicle Operator Services Agency.
- DVLA Medical Branch.
- Driving Standards Agency.
- Police.

Any medical condition that would affect a pupil's driving must be reported to the DVLA Medical Branch.

4.15 An instructor observes a driving fault committed by the pupil. This should be:
- used as a teaching point.
- used as a warning to the pupil.
- ignored and the lesson continued with.
- written down for later discussion.

Avoid retrospective comment and deal with the fault at the earliest opportunity. Use it as a teaching point to encourage a change for the better in the pupil.

4.16 'Rote' learning is a good method to use for:
- memorizing facts and figures.
- analysing a series of road manoeuvres.
- deciding on the best procedure at a roundabout.
- the reversing manoeuvres.

This can be a foundation on which to build knowledge and understanding. For example, a pupil can learn the braking distances by heart and quote them confidently. The more important aspect is that they put this theory into practice when driving.

4.17 The motivation and interest of a pupil having difficulty in learning can best be maintained by:
- giving a demonstration when mistakes are made.
- keeping strictly to the lesson plan.
- grading the tuition in short progressive steps with attainable goals.
- repeating exercises until they get it right.

When planning and delivering a training session it is important to structure development to suit pupil ability. Setting impossible targets or attempting to cover too much will do little for a pupil's confidence and probably demotivate them as well.

4.18 Initial assessment of a pupil before commencing instruction would normally be carried out in order to determine:
- the level at which instruction should begin.
- the range of general intelligence of the pupil.
- the length of instruction required for each pupil to complete the course.
- how often the pupil needs lessons.

When meeting a pupil with some previous driving experience, find out what they know and assess their driving on a suitable route. This will help to determine the needs and ability of the pupil.

4.19 From the trainee's point of view, a major advantage of being given learning objectives is that they:
- will have no need to ask questions of the instructor.
- can drive a vehicle with responsibility, concentration and patience.
- will know exactly what is expected of them and can evaluate their own progress.
- know when they are ready to take the test.

Stating clear and measurable objectives at the beginning of the lesson is a two-way process where the instructor explains what is to be achieved. The pupil then has an insight into what they are going to do. At the end of the lesson they are better placed to evaluate their progress and understand the feedback received from their instructor.

4.20 An instructor's expectations of their pupils are too high. This can:
- allow the pupils to progress at their own rate.
- provide reinforcement of learning.
- destroy the pupil's confidence.
- increase the pupil's confidence.

Everyone learns at different rates and instructors need to adapt their teaching to the ability of their pupil. Building confidence is an important part of teaching someone to drive and it can be hard to build but easy to lose.

4.21 The name given to the mental processes such as sensation and thinking is:
- cognitive.
- psychomotor.
- learning transfer.
- gestalt.

The mental approach and thought process applied to thinking things through are known as the cognitive domain of learning. This involves the thinking process, recall of information or making judgements and evaluations mentally.

4.22 Part of the MSM routine is referred to by the abbreviation PSL. These letters stand for:
- Position – Slow down – Lifesaver.
- Position – Signal – Look.
- Position – Speed – Look.
- Position – Speed – Lifesaver.

Regardless of driving experience, the Mirrors–Signal–Manoeuvre routine should become an integral part of driving. The manoeuvre part is broken down into: P – Position: position your vehicle correctly and in good time; S – Speed: adjust your speed as necessary for the pending manoeuvre; L – Look: look for other traffic or road users when you reach a point from when you can see. Assess the situation, then decide whether it is safe to proceed and act accordingly.

4.23 Ideally, in order to learn to drive it is necessary for pupils to:
- have acquired relevant basic knowledge of driving.
- want to learn.
- have specified aptitudes.
- fully understand the mechanics of the vehicle.

Delivering training at the pace that suits the pupil helps to build confidence and maintain a pupil's motivation to learn.

4.24 An instructor should tell their pupil that they must always look around before moving off:
- to check that there is no one in the blind spot.
- because it is expected.
- to avoid failing their driving test.
- or use their mirror(s) instead.

It is important that instructors explain that safety checks are not just a test requirement but are a vital part of keeping safe on the road. Explaining the reasons behind safety checks should help pupils to think for themselves and become safe drivers.

4.25 Instruction given in short progressive steps is likely to lead to:
- a sense of boredom by the pupil.
- sustained interest from the pupil.
- a lack of coordination in driving the vehicle.
- the completion of the lesson in a shorter time.

An interested pupil is likely to be well motivated and should retain information better than one who has lost interest. Everyone has different abilities, and instruction needs to be varied to suit the individual.

4.26 Lessons should be planned so that:
- they meet the needs and ability of the pupil.
- there are lots of mistakes made to exploit the pupil's weaknesses.
- there are lots of mistakes so that the instructor can be seen to give value for money.
- there are no mistakes made by the pupil to give them encouragement.

Some people find learning to drive easy while others struggle with the challenge. It is important that lessons are matched to the pupil's ability. Mismatching lessons and ability can lead to loss of confidence, and to disinterest and dissatisfaction.

4.27 An appropriate use of open questions is to establish a pupil's:
- attitudes to road procedures.
- level of practical knowledge.
- degree of psychomotor skills.
- motivation for learning to drive.

An ADI should encourage their pupils to talk about road procedures and give them the chance to think for themselves during these discussions. This will help the ADI to understand their pupils' attitude to driving and road safety and this in turn will influence the training of these aspects.

4.28 Feedback should be supplied to the pupil:
- only when the pupil makes a serious error.
- at some later stage when the pupil has a chance to relax.
- constructively for maximum impact.
- at the start of the next lesson.

ADIs should make every effort to build their pupil's confidence and constructive feedback plays an important part in this process.

4.29 Learning by rote is an effective method of:
- analysing a series of road manoeuvres.
- memorizing facts and figures.
- deciding on the best procedure at a roundabout.
- learning general driving.

In the early stages of learning to drive some learning by rote can be helpful. As skill develops, this learning needs to be applied appropriately and encouraging learners to do this independently should enable them to deal with any situation, even those they have not met before.

4.30 The process of perception can be described as:
- dealing with situations in retrospect.
- the interpretation of necessary information.
- the selective focusing on a given hazard.
- defining hazards as you pass them.

If a learner encounters a hazard they have never met before they may not perceive the level of danger that could arise or may not know the correct action to take. This lack of ability to interpret the information accurately is often due to a lack of experience, and is one of the reasons why new drivers are at greater risk than those with more experience.

4.31 You are about to return home from holiday when you become ill. A doctor prescribes drugs which are likely to affect your driving. You should:

- drive only if someone is with you.
- avoid driving on motorways.
- not drive yourself.
- never drive at more than 30 mph.

Find another way to get home even if this proves to be very inconvenient. You must not put other road users, your passengers or yourself at risk.

4.32 You take some cough medicine given to you by a friend. What should you do before driving?

- ask your friend if taking the medicine affected their driving.
- drink some strong coffee one hour before driving.
- check the label to see if the medicine will affect your driving.
- drive a short distance to see if the medicine is affecting your driving.

Never drive if you have taken drugs, without first checking what the side effects might be. They might affect your judgement and perception, and therefore endanger lives.

4.33 To reduce the volume of traffic on the roads you could:

- use a car with a smaller engine.
- share a car when possible.
- drive in a bus lane.
- travel by car at all times.

Walking or cycling are good ways to get exercise. Using public transport also gives the opportunity for exercise if you walk to the railway station or bus stop. Leave the car at home whenever you can.

4.34 You start to feel tired while driving. What should you do?

- increase your speed slightly.
- decrease your speed slightly.
- find a less busy route.
- pull over at a safe place to rest.

If you start to feel tired, stop at a safe place for a rest break. Every year many fatal incidents are caused by drivers falling asleep at the wheel.

4.35 Which of the following may help to deter a thief from stealing your car?

- always keeping the headlights on.
- fitting reflective glass windows.
- always keeping the interior light on.
- etching the car number on the windows.

Having your car registration number etched on all your windows is a cheap and effective way to deter professional car thieves.

4.36 When leaving your car, to help keep it secure you should:

- leave the hazard warning lights on.
- lock it and remove the key.
- park on a one-way street.
- park in a residential area.

Always remove the key and lock it when leaving your vehicle. Don't make it easy for thieves.

4.37 You have to leave valuables in your car. It would be safer to:

- put them in a carrier bag.
- park near a school entrance.
- lock them out of sight.
- park near a bus stop.

If you have to leave valuables in your car, always lock them out of sight. If you can see them, so can a thief.

4.38 During a lesson an instructor continually uses either the steering or the dual controls. This is likely to:

- build pupil confidence as they feel the instructor is in control.
- assist in developing the pupil's hazard awareness skills.
- do little to build the pupil's faith in the instructor.
- help to build up the pupil's anticipation skills.

If you need to use the dual controls, explain accordingly. Repeated use would strongly suggest that the pupil is out of their depth or the area is too difficult for their ability. Continuing in the same way will affect their confidence. The lesson plan should be adjusted to more aptly suit the pupil's needs and ability.

4.39 Which of the following types of glasses should *not* be worn when driving at night?
- half-moon.
- round.
- bi-focal.
- tinted.

If you are driving at night or in poor visibility, tinted lenses will reduce the efficiency of your vision, by reducing the amount of available light reaching your eyes.

4.40 Alcohol affects you because it:
- speeds up your reactions.
- increases your awareness.
- improves your coordination.
- reduces your concentration.

The safest rule is never drink and drive. Alcohol seriously affects judgement and concentration. It will reduce driving ability, give a false sense of confidence and slow down reactions.

Answers to these questions are in Chapter 9.

The explanations shown above in *italics* are the official DSA explanations. They do not comprise the complete knowledge that you need for proper understanding of the topic.

ADI Part 2 – own driving

04

ADI Part 2 exam – driving ability

This is the second part of the three-part qualifying exam for the ADI Register. The test consists of an eyesight test, followed by a practical test of your ability to drive to a very high standard.

The purpose of the test is to show whether you have a thorough understanding of good, up-to-date driving techniques and that you are capable of demonstrating these techniques in a practical way.

As previously indicated, remember that you are allowed only three attempts at this part of the ADI exam.

During the test you must show a high degree of skill and ability and you will be assessed on:

- the way you handle the controls of the car;
- your anticipation of the actions of other road users; the way you react to other people;
- your judgement of speed, distance and timing; consideration for the safety and comfort of road users, including your passengers;
- whether you drive in an environmentally friendly manner.

As part of the test you will be required to carry out various manoeuvres, including:

- moving away straight ahead or at an angle;
- overtaking, meeting or crossing the path of other vehicles and taking an appropriate course without undue hesitation;
- turning left- and right-hand corners correctly without undue hesitancy;
- stopping the vehicle as in an emergency;

- driving in reverse gear and while doing so entering a limited opening to the right and to the left;
- reverse parking into the space behind a parked car, within the space of about two car lengths and close to and parallel with the kerb;
- reverse parking into a parking bay;
- turning the vehicle round in the road by using forward and reverse gears.

Note: all these manoeuvres and exercises should be carried out 'with reasonable accuracy and using effective all-round observations'. You should not rely solely on mirrors during the exercises.

'Independent driving'

At some stage during the test you will be required to drive for about 10 minutes or so by following:

- traffic signs to a destination; or
- a series of verbal directions; or
- a combination of both.

To pass this part of the exam you must:

- drive to a high standard of competence;
- demonstrate the principles of eco-friendly driving;
- adhere to and attain national speed limits when safe and where possible;
- show a well-planned, positive, progressive drive.

Your personal driving skills must be of a very high standard – you should not be trying to drive merely as a perfect driver – the test is much more stringent than that.

The routes used by the DSA cover a variety of road and traffic conditions and will include dual carriageways and motorways where possible (depending on the location of the test centre used). Both rural and urban road conditions are included.

Application

You can book online at www.direct.gov.uk or by completing the letter from the DSA informing you of your theory test result. Alternatively you can phone DSA on 0300 200 1122 for assistance with the application.

A Welsh-language booking line is available on 0300 200 1133.

You can usually expect to wait about five to six weeks for an appointment, but waiting times vary from one centre to another, so you may find that it is more practical to offer a second alternative venue.

Fees

The current fee (December 2011) is £111. In Northern Ireland the fee is £130.

The car

You must provide a suitable vehicle that:

- is properly taxed and insured;
- has a valid MOT certificate if required;
- is a saloon or hatchback/estate car in proper working condition with front and rear seat belts in working order;
- is capable of the normal performance of vehicles of its type;
- has manual transmission (except for applicants with a disability);
- is right-hand drive;
- has a readily adjustable seat, with head restraint, for a forward-facing front-seat passenger;
- is not displaying L plates;
- is not fitted with a 'space-saver' tyre;
- has an additional, adjustable interior mirror for use by the examiner.

If your vehicle does not conform to any of these requirements the rest of the test will not be completed and you will lose the fee.

From time to time a member of the DSA staff may accompany your examiner to ensure the uniformity of the tests. All seat belts front and rear must therefore be in working order, otherwise the test might be cancelled. Anyone who accompanies you on test would also be expected to wear a seat belt.

Eyesight

At the start of the test you will be asked to read a standard vehicle registration plate from a distance of 26.5 metres, or 27.5 metres for a vehicle with the older-style number plate that has slightly wider letters and figures. During this test it is permissible for you to use spectacles or contact lenses.

Legal requirements for the eyesight test

The test is conducted 'in good daylight' conditions. If you need to use glasses or contact lenses you must keep them on for the practical driving part of the test.

If you fail the eyesight test the rest of the test will not take place. The test will be marked as a fail, you will lose the fee and the test will count as one of the three attempts allowed for of the practical tests.

Vehicle safety questions

At the start of the test and before the practical driving the examiner will ask several questions about basic vehicle safety. These questions are sometimes referred to as 'show me, tell me' as some questions require you to answer by demonstrating an actual vehicle check ('show me'), and others require an explanation of the condition or operation of various parts of the car ('tell me'). There are usually three 'tell me' questions and two 'show me'.

You might be asked questions on any of the following:

- tyres and brakes;
- steering;
- lights and reflectors;
- direction indicators;
- audible warning devices;
- fluids used in the engine, braking or steering system;
- coolants and lubrication;
- wipers, demisters, brake lights, fog lights, head restraints, ABS warning lights, correct operation of all relevant controls and switches.

Sample questions:

- 'Identify where you would check the engine oil level and tell me how you would check that the engine has sufficient oil.'
- '*Tell me* how you would check that the brakes are working before starting a journey.'
- '*Show me* how you would check that the power-assisted steering is working before starting a journey.'
- '*Show me* how you would check that the headlights and tail lights are working.'

Each incorrect answer is recorded as a *driving fault* up to a maximum of four faults. If all five questions are answered incorrectly a *serious fault* is recorded, meaning that you would fail.

The practical driving test

As with the practical L test, the examiner will explain a few of the 'ground rules' before you start the test. These will normally include:

- 'Follow the road ahead unless I give you an instruction to turn off.'
- 'I will tell you in good time if we are going to turn to the left or the right at a junction.'

- 'If you are unclear about any of my instructions, don't be afraid to ask – they will then be repeated or clarified.'
- 'Drive as you normally would – but remember that a high standard of competence is required.'

Preparation

To help prepare for the test you should make sure you have up-to-date copies of the DSA publications:

- *The Official Highway Code;*
- *Driving – the essential skills;*
- *Know Your Traffic Signs.*

You should also consider having some refresher training with an experienced and qualified tutor.

Training for the Part 2

Even if you have already passed an advanced driving test, the syllabus and style of driving of the other motoring organizations may differ from those of the DSA. It is therefore advisable to have an assessment with an experienced ADI tutor. While instructors at a local driving school may be extremely good at preparing candidates for the L test, they may not be fully conversant with the higher level of assessment required for this test.

Tutors registered under the ORDIT scheme know what the DSA's requirements are and are skilled at assessments at this level. They will be able to advise you on any adjustments needed to enhance your driving style and efficiency.

Even if you have been driving for many years, you may need to modify some aspects of your driving to streamline your performance in line with modern driving techniques. It is often said that 'unlearning' something you've been doing for years is far more difficult than learning something from scratch, so be aware that some experienced drivers find it difficult to adapt to a new style of driving.

Training with a qualified, experienced tutor is essential for several reasons:

- If you are still driving in the style you had been using for many years, you may be applying inefficient or outdated methods.
- Although you will have passed the theory test at this stage, there may still be some deficiencies in areas of your knowledge that could result in failure. A trained tutor will be able to identify these and teach you how to apply the rules and procedures correctly.
- The standard of driving required by the DSA is higher than that of some other advanced driving organizations.

- You may have some false assumptions about the test and its content – a good tutor will be able to advise you correctly.
- An assessment given under test conditions will be invaluable experience.
- The training you receive from your tutor will provide you with a demonstration of the teaching techniques you will need to acquire to become an effective instructor.

Failure is expensive, and it increases the pressure when attending for retests. In addition, if you do not take training with a specialist, you may well be at a disadvantage when it comes to taking your instructional ability test, as you will not have seen demonstrated the teaching skills you need to acquire. A good tutor will make an objective assessment of the current level of your personal driving skills and be able to guide you along the route to improvement and to explain why you might need to make changes to your style or methods.

You are allowed a maximum of three attempts at this test, so be prepared to invest in sufficient training.

It is sensible to have a couple of 'mock test' sessions with your tutor prior to taking the test just in case you have any last-minute doubts or queries, and need any advice or reassurance.

Syllabus

1a *Eyesight:*
You must be able to read a number plate from the prescribed distance. (See page 78.)

1b *Vehicle safety:*
You must be able to describe and demonstrate how to check the condition and safety of some of the car's components. (See page 79.)

1c *Highway Code:*
You must demonstrate that you can apply the rules.

2 *Controlled stop:*
You must be able to stop your vehicle safely, promptly and under full control. React promptly to the signal to stop. Keep both hands firmly on the wheel to maintain a straight line. Brake firmly and progressively as dictated by the road and weather conditions. Avoid braking so harshly that your car skids, or if your car has an anti-lock braking system, that it is activated. Remember you are supposed to be stopping under control.

You should be able to avoid skidding. If you feel the wheels start to lock up, release the brake momentarily and then reapply the pressure. Even if your vehicle has an ABS system, try to avoid braking so hard that it activates.

You will be stopped in a normal driving position so remember to check all around for other road users – particularly pedestrians and cyclists – before moving off again.

3, 4 and 5 *Reverse exercises:*

Reverse left into a limited opening:

Under control: taking account of any gradients; full control should be maintained throughout.

With proper observation: all-round checks should be made throughout and you should respond to the presence of other road users. This means giving priority when appropriate or proceeding if you are sure the other driver is waiting.

Reasonably accurately: you are an experienced driver; you should be able to maintain a reasonable degree of accuracy throughout the manoeuvre and finish in a safe position.

Reverse right into a limited opening:

Under control: as for the left reverse you should take account of any gradients, and maintain full control throughout.

With proper observation: as you will be manoeuvring on the wrong side of the road you will need to pay particular attention to the front, responding to the presence of other road users. This means giving them priority when appropriate.

Reasonably accurately: as an experienced driver, you may switch the focus of your observations from offside to rear to nearside in order to maintain a reasonable degree of accuracy. This will also help keep you up to date on the presence of others.

Reverse parking – either on the road or into a parking bay:

Under control: take account of any gradients, and maintain full control throughout.

With proper observation: as you may be manoeuvring into a more confined space from the middle of the road, you will need to pay particular attention to the presence of other road users. This means giving them priority when appropriate.

Reasonably accurately: whether reversing on the road or into a parking bay, you need to steer into the space accurately and finish up with your vehicle straight.

6 *Turn in the road:*

Under control: take account of any gradients, and maintain full control throughout, using the handbrake where necessary.

With proper observation: keep checking in all directions and give other road users priority when appropriate.

Reasonably accurately: you should be able to complete this manoeuvre in three movements. However, if the road is particularly narrow, you may need to take an extra movement.

All of your manoeuvres should be carried out efficiently – remember, you are an experienced driver.

7 *Take proper precautions before starting the engine:*

Make a habit of checking that the parking brake is secure and the gear lever is in neutral before starting the engine. However, if you happen to stall in an awkward situation and wish to get moving quickly, it is more efficient to keep your footbrake on, clutch down and switch on. You must, however, retain full control of your vehicle at all times.

8 *Control* – you should make proper use of:

Accelerator: progressive, gentle use and good accelerator sense should result in full control, a smooth ride and economical use of fuel. The accelerator should also be used smoothly and gently. Use 'accelerator sense' to begin the slowing-down process on the approach to hazards. This should avoid the need for last-minute harsh braking.

Clutch: use the clutch smoothly for moving off, stopping, changing up and down through the gears and for low speed manoeuvres. Avoid coasting after changing gear and when stopping.

Gears: use selective changing up and down the box to suit the circumstances and to achieve optimum fuel economy. Use gears to match the speed and power requirements dictated by the road and traffic conditions. Selective gear changing up and down the box will demonstrate that you are planning properly for hazards and driving economically.

Footbrake: push gently on the footbrake to begin with, gradually increasing the pressure and, to achieve a smooth stop, ease the pressure just before the car comes to a complete stop. The footbrake should be used gently and progressively. Plan well ahead for hazards and brake gently and in good time so that you can either proceed if the hazard clears, or you can come to a smooth stop in the correct place.

Parking brake: used for stops that are likely to last for more than a few seconds and where other traffic and pedestrians are present and, of course, to avoid rolling backwards or forwards on gradients. The handbrake should be used for stops that are likely to last for more than a few seconds or when parking.

Steering: an efficient method should be used to give maximum efficiency, leverage and control. Use the steering smoothly. Using the whole wheel and looking where you want to go should help avoid under- or over-steering when cornering.

Use all the foot controls progressively and smoothly.

9   *Move off:*

Safely: make full all-round observations to ensure that no other road users will be affected when you move off.

Under control: maintain full control when moving away in all situations – level, uphill, downhill and at an angle.

Check all the mirrors and blind areas before moving off. You need to cover all of those areas to the sides and rear of your car that are not seen in the mirrors. You are checking, for example, for traffic emerging from side roads and driveways, or cyclists or pedestrians who may be crossing the road diagonally behind you.

Signal only if it will be of benefit to another road user, including pedestrians. This will show that you are looking and thinking effectively.

Move off smoothly and under control in all circumstances by coordinating the hand and foot controls, handbrake and steering. For moving off downhill use the footbrake and clutch effectively to avoid coasting

10   *Use of the mirrors well before:*

Signalling: check mirrors well before making any decision to signal so that discrimination is effective and signals are timed correctly.

Changing direction: no action to change direction should be taken unless you are sure that you will not be affecting another road user.

Changing speed: always be sure of the all-round situation before changing your speed, whether you are speeding up or slowing down.

Use the Mirrors–Signal–Manoeuvre (MSM) routine effectively.

Using all of the mirrors effectively means constantly taking into account what is happening all around you and acting safely so that you don't inconvenience any other road user. Apply the MSM routine and check your mirrors well before reaching any hazard and before slowing down, signalling and changing direction. By doing this you will be better placed to decide whether or not a signal will be helpful and when to time it.

11   *Give signals by direction indicators/arm:*

Where necessary: if any other road user (including pedestrians) would benefit from a signal, use one. If appropriate, that is, if you have time and your window is open, consider giving an arm signal for stopping at a zebra crossing if you think an oncoming driver or pedestrian might benefit. The horn should be used as a warning of your presence and can be helpful when you are approaching a blind bend or summit.

Correctly: use only signals that clearly show your intentions to move off, stop or change direction.

Properly timed: time your signals so as not to confuse other road users. For example, if you are waiting to move away from the kerb and vehicles are approaching from the rear, too early a signal may make the other drivers think that you are likely to pull out in front of them. If you are taking a second road on the left, make sure you time your signal so as not to encourage a driver waiting in the first one to emerge in front of you. You should also remember that early positioning helps confirm your intentions, for example when passing parked vehicles where you could consider that a signal is not needed.

Use the signals shown in the Highway Code when they will be helpful to inform any other road user (including pedestrians) of your intentions. Use signals in good time so that other people have time to respond; and make sure you cancel the signal after the manoeuvre. Avoid giving a signal when it might cause confusion. For example, using a right signal for passing a line of parked vehicles where there is also a right turn.

12   *Clearance/obstructions:*

When there are obstructions in the road, be prepared to slow down or stop and give way to oncoming vehicles. As you pass parked vehicles, give plenty of clearance, allowing for children running out from between them, doors opening or drivers pulling out without warning.

Where there are parked vehicles, work out whose priority it should be, but also anticipate what the oncoming driver is likely to do. Priorities do not really matter if the other driver is determined to take the road space. Sometimes it is courteous to make a positive decision to give way, for example if you are travelling downhill and there is a larger vehicle coming up the hill towards you.

13   *Response to signs and signals – take appropriate action on all:*

Traffic signs: road signs are there for your information and guidance. Respond to them early by checking your mirrors and taking the appropriate action. Check for signs whenever you are approaching a different type of road, and make sure you are always aware of the speed limit for the road you are using.

Road markings: are also for your guidance. Look and plan well ahead, and respond to hazard warning lines by checking your mirrors and looking for any possible dangers. Plan early for any lane changes so that you do not have to take any late action that might affect others. Be aware of any stop lines and make sure you bring your vehicle to a complete stop.

Traffic lights: plan your approach according to the colour already showing – remember they could change at any moment. If the lights are on green, check your mirrors, adjust your speed and be prepared to stop until you reach that point of no return when it would be unsafe to stop. Demonstrate that you know the meaning of amber. If, when it shows, you are so close to the line that you would need to brake sharply to stop, you should continue – particularly if someone is close behind you. If red is showing, check your mirrors, adjust your speed and be prepared to stop if it remains on red, or to change to an appropriate gear and proceed if it changes to green.

Signals given by traffic controllers: obey any signals given by authorized persons such as police officers or school patrol wardens.

Other road users: although most drivers use signals correctly, some do not! If an approaching driver is signalling to turn into your road, make sure that they are actually going to turn. Similarly, if other drivers flash their headlights at you to proceed, do not just go without checking all-round safety for yourself.

You should constantly scan the road well ahead, looking for all signs, road markings and traffic lights. Plan ahead and work out what might happen at traffic lights. Try to anticipate any changes and have your car under full control so that you can either stop comfortably or proceed safely. Remember that a green light means 'Go if it's safe.' Check in all directions as you proceed through any junctions. Obey signals given by police officers, traffic wardens and school patrols. React promptly to signals given by other road users, including those in charge of animals. Remember some drivers use unofficial signals – check all around for yourself before proceeding.

14 *Use of speed:*

Speed limits are maximum speeds. Although you should make proper progress, your speed should be dictated not only by the limit for the road you are on, but also by the weather, the condition of the road surface, the traffic volume and any pedestrian activity.

Taking into account the road, weather and traffic conditions, and any road signs and speed limits, make safe and reasonable progress. Remember that a speed limit is the maximum allowed for the road you are travelling along. There are many times when you may need to be travelling much more slowly, for example when driving past schools where there may be children about.

15 *Following distance:*

Always keep a safe distance between yourself and the vehicle ahead of you. If the vehicle in front of you stops, you should have time to take action without getting too close to it. Leave a gap of at least a metre for every mph of your speed – or use the two-second rule. In very wet conditions, you will need at least twice this distance. If someone is following you too closely, drop back even further. This will allow you to give the following driver more time to stop, because you will be allowing for their stopping distance as well as your own. Keep even further back when following large vehicles, as it will give you a better view of the road ahead, particularly if you are considering overtaking.

By applying the two-second rule you should be able to stop comfortably.

16 *Maintain progress:*

Drive at a realistic speed appropriate to the road and traffic conditions. Approach all hazards at a safe and controlled speed, without being overcautious or interfering with the progress of other traffic. Plan well ahead and take opportunities to proceed at all types of junction as soon as you can see that it's safe to go.

When you have to stop, keep looking in all directions for a suitable gap in the traffic and have your car ready to move smoothly into it, building up your speed and changing up efficiently so as not to affect any other road user.

17 *Junctions (including roundabouts):*

Speed on approach: try to time your arrival at junctions in accordance with the sightlines. That is, if the junction is opening up, without slowing down excessively, give yourself time to start making early observations. If your sightlines are very restricted, do not waste too much time on the approach if you will not be able to see until you get there!

Observations: you cannot make any safe decision to proceed until you have looked properly in all directions. On the approach to T junctions, as soon as sightlines begin to open up (no matter in which direction), start looking and keep looking in both directions until you are absolutely sure you will not affect another road user. At crossroads, keep looking in all directions – even when you have priority. Remember, even a green light does not give you 100 per cent safety – check there's no one proceeding through on the wrong colour.

Approaching traffic: your actions should never make another driver slow down or change direction. Before you make any decision to cross another driver's path, make sure you have enough time and, just as importantly, make sure you know what is happening in the new road.

Turning right: when turning from main roads into a side road, position your car close to the centre of the road to avoid holding up the following traffic. Make sure you know what is happening in the new road before you commit yourself to turning in. When emerging from wide roads, position yourself just to the left of the centre line so as not to impede the flow of left-turning traffic. However, if the road is narrow, keep farther to the left to allow more room for vehicles turning in.

Turning left: whether turning in or emerging, maintain your normal driving position, about a metre from the kerb, to allow plenty of room for the rear wheels to clear the kerb.

Cutting corners: make sure you position correctly, according to the width of the road, and if you have to wait for oncoming traffic, that you wait just short of the point of turn. This should ensure that you turn in on your own side of the road, avoiding cutting corners. However, if there are parked vehicles near the end of the road making an ideal turn impossible, move a little further forward before turning, to give you a better view.

Junction notes:

- Apply the MSM routine early.
- Check for signs and road markings.
- Take up an appropriate position for your intended direction.
- Your approach speed should be such that you can either proceed if it's safe, or stop comfortably when necessary.
- Maintain a safe position throughout by avoiding cutting right corners or swinging out on left turns.
- At roundabouts demonstrate good lane discipline and watch for other vehicles cutting into your lane.
- Before turning at junctions, check for cyclists or motorcyclists on your left, and for pedestrians crossing the road.
- At some junctions, where the view is restricted, you may need to 'creep and peep' before you can make effective observations. Check for other clues by taking advantage of reflections in shop windows, telephone boxes, or by looking through other vehicles' windows. Do not proceed until you are absolutely sure that you can see far enough to make a safe decision to go.

18 *Judgement:*

Allow adequate clearance to stationary vehicles and obstructions. Allow sufficient room for doors opening, drivers moving off without signalling or people walking between vehicles. This means you should, in ideal circumstances, be allowing about a metre's clearance.

Meeting other traffic: when the width of the road is restricted, be prepared to give way, no matter whose priority it may be. Remember, the oncoming driver may not be as courteous as you are! If there are vehicles parked on both sides, but there is room to proceed through, then allow an equal amount of clearance to both sides – in other words, drive down the centre of the road. On roads where there is a need to maintain the traffic flow but you cannot give the ideal clearance, then slow down and drive through cautiously, allowing time to respond if the situation changes. You may also need to give way to an oncoming vehicle even when it should be your priority! It's also easier for you to give way if you're travelling downhill, particularly to larger vehicles.

Overtaking: this is potentially *the* most dangerous manoeuvre! Before you decide to overtake you should ask yourself, *Is it safe, legal and necessary?*

Make sure you know what's happening behind you and that you can see far enough ahead so you know you'll have sufficient time to complete the manoeuvre quickly and efficiently without affecting any other road user. Allow plenty of room when overtaking cyclists and motorcyclists in case they wobble or swerve. After overtaking make sure you allow plenty of room before pulling in again.

Crossing the path of other traffic: never rush to beat an oncoming vehicle when turning right. If you have to rush, there is a risk involved, and you should never put yourself into a situation your eyes have not visited first.

When turning right and it's not busy, look and plan well ahead. Try to time your arrival so that you can keep moving. However, make sure you do have plenty of time! If there are oncoming vehicles, you should not make them slow down, swerve or stop so that you can make your turn.

19   Positioning:

Normally position your vehicle well to the left. On a road of reasonable width, your normal driving position should be about a metre from the kerb – or even a little farther out if there are large puddles and pedestrians around. If there are lots of parked vehicles, maintain a position to pass them all unless there are junctions on the right where vehicles may emerge.

Give cycle lanes the same distance. On narrower roads, in rural areas for example, you may have to drive a little nearer the edge of the road, in which case you will need to adjust your speed according to the situation and the presence of any other road users. On left bends, keep to the centre of your lane to maintain safety from oncoming vehicles. On right bends, keep to the left to improve your view.

Driving in lanes: exercise lane discipline and drive in the centre of your lane, avoiding straddling the lines. Look and plan ahead and select your lane early. When a lane change is necessary, apply the MSM routine early, carrying out the manoeuvre safely and gradually. When driving in lanes, keep well to the centre so that you don't straddle the markings.

20   Pedestrian crossings:

Dealing with the light-controlled crossings is relatively straightforward, as you have to obey the light sequences. Anticipate when they are likely to change and apply the MSM routine in good time. Stop at the stop line and secure your car with the parking brake.

At *zebra crossings,* it can be slightly more complicated. You need to be on the lookout for pedestrians likely to step out at any moment. Look and plan well ahead, apply the MSM routine and always be travelling at a speed at which you can stop within the distance you can see is clear. Be patient and only proceed when you know it is safe. Pedestrians have priority anywhere in the road – be ready to anticipate their actions and, if possible, give them time to get onto the pavement.

At *toucan crossings,* be prepared to give way to cyclists as well as pedestrians.

You should be aware of the different types of crossing and show consideration to all groups of pedestrians.

Your speed on the approach should be appropriate to:

- the type of crossing;
- traffic and road conditions;
- pedestrian activity.

Whatever the type of crossing you are approaching, if there are any pedestrians using it you must stop.

Where a police officer, traffic warden or school patrol is controlling the traffic, you must obey their signals.

Before moving off, check all around for pedestrians and cyclists.

21   *Position/normal stops:*

Drivers who are under test conditions sometimes feel they must stop as soon as they are asked to do so! However, you must make sure that you only stop where it is safe, legal and convenient. Remember, you should be demonstrating that you know and understand the rules by applying them correctly. As an experienced driver, you should know where it's legal, safe and convenient to park without causing problems for others.

Look and plan ahead and choose a suitable place for stopping, taking into consideration any signs, road markings, openings/driveways, junctions. Stop close to the edge of the road.

22   *Awareness and planning:*

Pedestrians: people do not always do as they should, and pedestrians do not normally read *The Highway Code.* Always expect the unexpected and, in any area where there is pedestrian activity, try to anticipate what might happen. Check your mirrors and be ready to slow down or stop.

Cyclists: give as much clearance as you can to cyclists. They are unpredictable and could wobble into your path at any time, particularly in windy conditions. Expect them to ride off pavements without warning and to cycle in between lanes. Always check to your sides before moving off in queues of traffic.

Drivers: these are pedestrians on wheels – they do not always act as they should. That they know the rules does not mean they will always apply them. Look and plan all around, watching out and allowing for drivers moving off, changing lanes or stopping suddenly; cutting corners; turning across your path; taking priority when it should be yours; not using signals correctly; following you too closely; not obeying traffic signs and signals.

You can only anticipate events if you are constantly scanning ahead and all around and making effective use of the information you are gathering. You should:

- consider what is happening on the road;
- take account of the traffic and weather conditions;
- anticipate what might happen;
- take early action to maintain full control of your vehicle.

You should also:

- judge what other road users are going to do;
- predict how their actions are going to affect you;
- take early action to avoid problems and conflict.

In particular you should consider the more vulnerable groups of road user, such as:

- young, old or infirm pedestrians;
- cyclists and motorcyclists;
- people with animals.

23   *Ancillary controls:*

You should maintain constant all-round visibility in your car. Without needing to look down at the controls, use the washer/wipers, demisters and fan as necessary. If you use the air conditioning, make sure you switch it off if you open your window – this includes during any of the manoeuvre exercises. For normal driving, having the windows open in hot weather causes drag and will use more fuel than the air-conditioning unit does.

You should understand the function of all of your car's controls and switches.

Make sure you always maintain full visibility and operate your vehicle in safety.

When needed, you should be able to locate and operate ancillary controls without looking at them.

Marking system

This test demands a high level of driving skill and, as a result, the marking system is more critical than on other tests such as the L test. Faults are assessed under three categories:

1 Driving faults – errors that detract from the 'perfect' drive.

2 Serious or potentially dangerous faults – faults that cause potential danger or damage, and in different circumstances could lead to a serious situation arising.

3 Dangerous faults – faults that cause actual danger.

To pass this part of the exam you must have no serious or dangerous faults and a maximum of six driving faults.

Examples of different types of fault:

Driving faults:
- ineffective use of the mirrors and lack of response;
- making too many unnecessary gear changes;
- signalling incorrectly; lack of observations during manoeuvre exercises.

Serious or potentially dangerous faults:
- failure to respond to the presence of other road users during a manoeuvre exercise;
- cutting a right corner with no other road user present.

Dangerous faults:
- turning right across the path of an oncoming vehicle;
- emerging from a junction and slowing down another driver;
- driving too slowly for the conditions and missing opportunities to proceed in busy situations.

Eco driving

In the Part 2 ADI exam you are expected to be an experienced driver and will need to show that you are aware of the need for fuel efficiency and an environmentally friendly approach in all aspects of your driving. As an ADI you will need to be able to encourage your new drivers in the use of all these various techniques. Fuel-efficient driving is now part of the ADI Part 2 exam as well as the L driver test.

Eco-friendly driving can make a significant impact on the global use of conventional fuels and make a positive contribution to the reduction of carbon emissions. This process starts with an awareness of the availability of vehicles with alternative fuels such as electric and 'dual fuel' power.

To make an improvement in fuel efficiency, you can consider several areas of your own style of driving, including:

- *Acceleration.* Your use of acceleration should be steady, smooth and progressive whenever possible, avoiding unnecessary speed peaks. A smooth driving style can save up to 10 per cent of fuel used. Where appropriate, use the cruise control, as this can be more efficient on fuel usage.

- *Braking.* Any use of the footbrake should be smooth and positive, with a certain amount of tapering on and off. Avoid any harsh use of the brakes by easing off the accelerator earlier where possible.

- *Gear changes.* Make gear changes effectively, with block changes up and down where appropriate. Move into the higher gears reasonably quickly. Cars with manual gear change are more fuel efficient than automatics.

- *Hazard awareness* and forward planning techniques should be used effectively to minimize any unnecessary or harsh changes of speed or direction.

- *Vehicle sympathy.* Keep engine speeds relatively low whenever possible. Generally, keeping the engine speed to about 3,000 rpm can save a considerable amount of fuel. Use all vehicle controls smoothly to avoid any unnecessary sharp fluctuations in speed.

- *Manoeuvring.* Reversing into a parking space and then driving out forwards is generally regarded as more fuel efficient than reversing out when the engine is cold.

- *Speed.* Keep to all legal speed limits and plan well ahead for any changes. Some experts reckon that reducing your top speed by 10 mph can save a considerable amount of fuel.

- *Air conditioning.* Avoid using air conditioning or climate control unless it is necessary, as this can be detrimental to fuel consumption. Avoid driving with the car windows or sunroof open, as this can create 'drag' and an increase in fuel consumed.

Individually, these savings may not seem much, but collectively they can make substantial reductions, not only on your own costs but also on the global use of carbon fuels.

Eco driving – marking

Eco-safe driving faults are marked on the DL25 as a 'driving fault' by the examiner, using one of the spare boxes on the form.

The main areas that the examiner will be looking for include:

- Hazard awareness and planning: hazards are identified at an early stage, giving adequate time to respond and to decelerate as appropriate.

- Speed limits: complied with all legal speed limits. Speed is appropriate to all road, traffic and weather conditions.
- Starting up and moving off: avoids excessive use of the accelerator. Moves off promptly and smoothly.
- Accelerator: used smoothly. Accelerator was properly coordinated with the other controls.
- Gears: used efficiently and effectively, with the appropriate gear engaged at all times.
- Engine braking: used effectively to take advantage of engine braking power where appropriate.
- Engine power and torque: utilized higher gears at lower engine speed where appropriate without causing the engine to labour.
- Cruise control: used in appropriate situations, but without compromising road safety.

Remember – this is not just about saving fuel in your vehicle; it is also to do with releasing fewer polluting chemicals into the atmosphere and conserving fuels globally.

The result

At the end of the test the examiner will offer a debrief on all your driving faults. If you wish, your trainer is allowed to be present, but must not take part in the discussion. The examiner will then give you a copy of the test report together with some explanatory notes and a letter confirming the result.

What next?

When you pass you will find an application form for the Part 3 exam on the back of the result letter. Don't send this off until you are absolutely sure you are ready to take the practical instruction ability part of the exam.

You will also receive a trainee licence application form. A trainee licence can help you gain experience in instructing before you consider taking the Part 3 exam.

Full details of the trainee licence are in Chapter 6.

Finally, on the day of the test:

- Make sure the car is clean (inside and out!).
- Check windscreen washers, lights, indicators.
- Spare bulbs?
- Aim to arrive early at the test centre.
- Allow for any traffic delays on the way.
- Allow time for a 'comfort break'.

- Familiarize yourself with the venue, where to park and the immediate area.
- Make sure you have the necessary documents with you.

And take with you:

- bottle of water and sweets;
- training aids and pens, pencils;
- reference books;
- spectacles/sunglasses;
- cleaning cloth and duster.

Remember, you may only have three attempts at this test. If you fail on the third, and still wish to continue with the qualifying process, you will have to wait until a two-year period elapses from passing the theory/hazard perception test. You will then have to start the whole process again by taking Part 1.

Driving theory

05

When you are preparing for the ADI driving test you will be aiming to use an effective, economical and safe method of driving. To do this you need to know and understand the theory behind good driving principles. However, as driving is mainly a practical skill, these principles can be developed only through effective practice and experience. It involves a complex mixture that combines:

- knowledge;
- understanding;
- awareness;
- attitude.

In order to practise 'safe driving for life' in your own driving you need to identify all these elements.

It is extremely unlikely that 'the perfect driver' exists. However, perfection is something that we should all try to achieve. In striving for perfection, we need to recognize some of the main ingredients and characteristics of 'the perfect driver', which include skill, knowledge and attitude elements

Skill

To become a completely skilful driver you should be in total control of the car at all times. All your actions should be smooth, positive and precise. The vehicle should:

- be in the correct position on the road;
- be travelling at a safe speed for the road and traffic conditions;
- have an appropriate gear engaged to suit the speed and power requirements.

Observation, anticipation and forward planning – all of which require total concentration – are essential at all times. Your driving ability is not judged solely on manoeuvring and control skills, but also on the skill to read the road and traffic conditions effectively and to take account of what other road users may do.

Knowledge

As an experienced driver you will need to know and understand the laws, rules and regulations relating to road procedure. Without this knowledge, even the most skilful driver cannot become completely effective. It is generally accepted that knowledge generates positive attitudes.

Attitude

Knowledge of the subject and skill in handling the car are not sufficient qualities in themselves. They need to be applied in a safe, sensible manner. This means taking into account mistakes other drivers make and being prepared to make allowances for them.

Attitudes have a profound effect on the quality of driving, and although relatively easy to define in general terms, they are more difficult to assess in the individual driver. Remember that you should always be trying to drive in a considerate, courteous and tolerant manner to other road users.

Attitude influences the behaviour of drivers, with reckless or unsafe actions being attributed to a negative one. Opinions are not always objective when judgements are made about a traffic situation or another driver. Judgement in any situation may be influenced by attitudes acquired previously in a similar event. An inappropriate or negative attitude can sometimes make drivers see things not as they actually are, but as they imagine them to be.

Motivation describes the personal needs and drives of the individual. It ranges from the need to survive to a feeling of well-being and achievement of desires. Motivation can be used in a positive way to improve driver behaviour. However, it can sometimes cause illogical and potentially unsafe driving. For example, drivers may take uncharacteristic risks if they:

- are late for work or an important appointment;
- want to get the better of another driver;
- wish to demonstrate a superiority of skill;
- are trying to gain the admiration of friends or passengers.

Emotion is the general term used to describe feelings such as love, hate or fear. Intense emotions like anger, frustration and grief tend to turn the focus of the mind in on itself. This in turn lowers the attention being paid to the driving task and limits perceptive abilities.

Anger may result from an argument. Frustration may result from being held up behind a slow-moving vehicle. Anxiety may be the result of worries about work or other personal problems.

Driving is in itself a stressful activity, and deficient knowledge or skill can result in frustration and may generate destructive emotions.

Perception is the brain's interpretation of information it receives from the eyes, ears and other senses. The perception of a particular traffic hazard is carried out by the primary information-processing functions of the brain. This involves a need to compare the current situation with existing knowledge and previous experience.

Hazard recognition requires an active and rapid assessment of the potential risks involved in a particular situation, and the driver must anticipate events before they occur. This anticipation relies heavily on stored memories of similar experiences.

Perception is the driver's visual and mental awareness, and it provides information on:

- speed;
- position;
- timing.

As drivers we have limited perceptual capacity and are often faced with an overload of information from everything that is going on around us on the roads. In order to maintain safety when this happens, it becomes necessary to prioritize. This means that the important pieces of information will need to be attended to while other aspects will have to be ignored.

Road sense

Driving is a continuous process of observing, responding and attending to constantly changing needs involving the vehicle, the road layout and traffic conditions. You need to continually recognize, assess and reassess hazards and respond correctly in good time. These responses involve the MSM (mirrors–signal–manoeuvre) and PSL (position–speed–look) routines.

Within the individual elements of these routines, you should:

- look, assess and decide what action can safely be taken in relation to the information received from the all-round situation;
- look, assess and decide whether a signal is required;
- assess whether the signal is having the required effect on others;
- look, assess and decide what effect any changes in position and speed are likely to have on others;
- decide what further observations or actions may be required.

To be an efficient driver you need to assess the part you are taking in the changing road and traffic environment. For example, you should not only respond to developing situations, but you should also see yourself as an active part of those situations – often contributing to them. Assessing risks and deciding on the appropriate response to a hazard involve a continuous process of assessing and reassessing the constantly changing traffic situation. This means:

- assessing the degree of risk;
- deciding on the priorities;
- focusing attention on the most important aspect;
- deciding on a specific course of action;
- responding in good time;
- reassessing.

Anticipation is having the ability to predict the actions of other road users and is part of the visual search skills. You need to know:

- why, where and when you must look;
- the kind of things to look for;
- what to expect;
- how to see effectively as opposed to just 'looking'.

Risk assessment is influenced by knowledge and previous experience. It can be learnt on a trial-and-error basis or through controlled exercises. Most drivers will recognize that there is a bend in the road; however, they might not all think of the possibility of there being an obstruction hidden from view.

Visual awareness

As an experienced driver you will be constantly gathering information from the all-round traffic scene. An active visual scan not only provides more information at an earlier stage, but also gives more time to respond. The eye movements of experienced drivers need to be very rapid, moving quickly from one point of interest to another, checking and rechecking areas of risk. Try to practise an effective visual search system that involves:

- looking well ahead – allowing you to steer a safe and smooth line;
- keeping the eyes moving – to help you build up a more complete picture and improve awareness;
- getting the big picture – looking all around assists with the judgement of speed and position;
- allowing others to see you – positioning your car so that you can see and be seen;
- looking for alternatives – working out an action plan that may be required if events change.

Hazard recognition

The natural inclination of many drivers is to keep going, unless it is obviously unsafe, for example by steering away from a moving hazard rather than slowing down to avoid it. You need to:

- actively search the road ahead;
- assess the safety of proceeding;
- recognize the consequences of your actions.

When you are reading the road ahead don't just wait for something to happen; be ready to anticipate that something might happen and respond in good time so that you attempt to avoid any potential problems. To do this you need to obtain as much relevant information about the road and traffic situation as you can. For example:

- To steer accurately and adjust to safe speeds before reaching a hazard, look well ahead for bends, gradients, road signs, junctions and obstructions such as parked cars, road works and traffic hold-ups.
- To maintain tyre and road surface adhesion, drive smoothly and approach hazards at a suitable speed, taking into account weather conditions, road surface and any camber on bends.
- To anticipate and act on the actions of other road users, scan the road for anything with a potential for moving into or across your path.
- To be able to stop well within the distance you can see to be clear, you need to identify any blind areas and adjust your speed accordingly.
- To avoid problems with road users to your sides and rear, make full use of all of the mirrors and use your peripheral vision. You also need a good understanding of the principles of communicating with other road users.

Making decisions

Some drivers' decisions often polarize between deciding whether to stop or go in situations where neither is necessarily the correct decision. Inadequate information and hurried assessments are often major causes of incorrect decisions. Try to make decisions early enough to create extra time and leave you with alternatives. For example, when you are approaching a parked vehicle where there is a line of slow-moving traffic approaching from the opposite direction, there could be three choices:

1 It is safe to proceed.
2 It is unsafe to go now.
3 We need more information to reassess the situation before a decision can be made.

Any decision – whether it is to proceed, hold back, give way or stop – must be continually reassessed. Make your assessments in advance and keep all options open. For example, when approaching a green traffic light you should be anticipating the possibility of it changing and be ready with the decision to stop. At some point on the approach, however, you will be too close to pull up safely, and the only safe decision is to continue. When approaching any traffic lights, no matter what colour is showing, you need to continually reassess what to do if they change.

Response and control skills

Communication

Methods of communication between road users are complex, and involve much more than merely using the commonly recognized means of signalling by using:

- indicators;
- brake lights;
- arm signals;
- horn;
- flashing headlights;
- hazard warning flashers.

An effective communication system involves:

- the position of the vehicle on the road;
- the speed of the vehicle;
- implied signals of intent;
- eye contact;
- courtesy signals and acknowledgements.

Signalling by position

In general, the driver who maintains a correct course, speed and position on the road should not need to signal. Although this is not completely valid for all circumstances, there is an element of truth to it, and you can often anticipate an intended act from another vehicle's position.

Taking up the correct position will help to confirm your signals. Where the position does not appear to confirm a signal, other drivers may become confused. For example, a vehicle may be signalling left, but if the car's position is more towards the centre of the road, other drivers may understandably become confused as they are receiving conflicting information.

Signalling by speed

Changes in speed can also be used as an indication of a driver's intended action. For example, in a situation where a vehicle is signalling to turn left, is positioned correctly and is obviously slowing down, there is a combination of evidence to suggest a left turn will be made, and other road users do not have to rely on one single factor.

Other examples of where speed clearly signals another driver's intentions are when a car is approaching a junction far too quickly for it to give way, and when a driver is accelerating rather than slowing down near a zebra crossing. By slowing down well before crossings, you can clearly signal your intentions to the pedestrians waiting to cross as well as letting any other drivers know what you are doing.

Defensive signals

These are the signals you might use to warn other road users of your presence. They include the use of flashing headlights, the horn and hazard warning lights. The use of the horn would normally be considered in relatively slow-moving traffic conditions. Use it when you think another road user might not be aware of your presence, for example when approaching blind summits, sharp bends on narrow roads, or when you see vehicles reversing from driveways. On higher-speed roads, such as motorways, flashing the headlights would be more effective because the noise of traffic can drown the sound of the horn,

Use the hazard warning lights only when stationary or in an emergency, unless you are coming to a stop for a traffic hold-up on a motorway.

Implied signals, eye contact and courtesy

Try to recognize and interpret the speed and movement of other traffic and to be alert to implied or potential movement, for example the pedestrians standing at the edge of the pavement near a zebra crossing.

A vehicle waiting at a give-way line always has the potential to move into your path. Treat these implications with respect and be ready to slow down.

Eye contact is another important form of communication. For example, when you are slowing down on the approach, or waiting at a pedestrian crossing, it helps to reassure pedestrians they have been seen; or when you are waiting to pull into a line of slow-moving traffic it may persuade others to hang back and allow you to move out into the traffic stream.

Speed adjustment

The senses used in the judgement of speed are sight, hearing, balance and touch.

The interpretation of speed can be very difficult at times, particularly in a modern car with a sound-insulated interior. In the absence of vibration and noise on a smooth road that has no nearby side features such as buildings, speed can seem deceptively slow.

Speed is usually assessed through a combination of factors that involve an established speed 'norm' learnt from previous experiences. It can be judged from:

- the rate at which visual images disappear to the sides;
- road, wind and engine noise;
- the sense of balance when changing speeds and direction;
- the general 'feel' of the vehicle on the road;
- comparisons with established 'speed norms'.

These speed norms can sometimes be misleading, for example when approaching the intersection at the end of the slip road after leaving a motorway.

Speed adjustments are required to maintain sufficient safety margins so that you can stop well within the distance you can see to be clear and in accordance with the traffic conditions, visibility and regulations. These adjustments must take into account the critical perceptual and attention overload limitations of any driver.

As your speed increases your visual point of focus needs to be farther ahead, while there will be a corresponding reduction in your peripheral vision. Where you need to attend to foreground detail, you must reduce your speed. Peripheral vision will assist in the judgement of your speed and position. If you do not reduce your speed you may well miss important risk factors, and your awareness of lateral position and safety margin will be limited.

To attain maximum awareness you need to apply an active visual scanning process for observing the road and traffic environment in its entirety, including signs, markings and traffic flow. By using this scanning process, and by maintaining proper control of your speed, you should be able to maintain a safe course while at the same time watching for the potential movement of other road users and compensating for them in good time.

You should always be travelling at a speed at which you can stop safely within the distance you can see to be clear. This means also taking into consideration how closely you are being followed. If a driver is far too close for comfort, you will need to take responsibility for their safety as well as your own. To do this you should:

- ease off the gas gradually;
- drop back from the vehicle ahead;
- look and plan as far ahead as possible;
- slow down early, braking gently when you see a hazard.

By allowing more space between you and the vehicle ahead, and braking early and gently, you will be creating more time for the following driver to respond.

Position

As well as being in the correct position in relation to the type of road and any change in direction you may be considering, you also need to consider your distance from the vehicle ahead. Positioning properly, safely and with consideration involves:

- your driving position in the road;
- driving in the centre of your lane;
- changing lanes early and gradually;
- allowing sufficient safety cushion between you and the vehicle ahead;
- allowing sufficient safety margins when passing parked vehicles or other obstructions;
- maintaining safety margins that will allow for the unexpected movement of others;
- selecting safe parking positions;
- taking up suitable positions on the approach to junctions so that you can take effective observations;
- positioning correctly when turning so that minimum disruption is caused to the traffic flow.

To position yourself correctly in order to maintain good sightlines and visibility of the road ahead, you need to position out towards the centre of the road when approaching parked vehicles, and be prepared, when giving way to oncoming traffic, to wait well back from the obstruction.

Other considerations when waiting in traffic include not obstructing crossings or access to side roads and entrances, and not stopping so close to the vehicle ahead as to be unable to pull out around it should the need arise.

Gathering information

Failing to take precautionary measures in doubtful situations can often result in the situation becoming critical and making extreme measures necessary. Before making any commitment to act, you need to gather relevant information so that you can deal with any situation safely and effectively.

Driving is not just a series of decisions to stop or go. In many situations you will need to put into effect an information-gathering exercise. For this, you will need to slow down to create time for the situation to develop, and keep your options open before making a definite commitment to keep moving or stop. Take precautionary measures when your vision is restricted or where there may be an unseen hazard, for example over the brow of a hill or around a bend.

Hold-back procedure

There are various ways of holding back from problems, including momentarily easing off the accelerator to maintain a safe gap. Maintaining safety where there are hazards normally means:

- looking and planning well ahead;
- anticipating any changing circumstances and potential hazards;
- maintaining good vehicle control at all times;
- slowing down early enough to hold back from the hazard.

Hold-back procedure involves actively reducing the speed with a view to looking, deciding or waiting, and maintaining safe options in moments of uncertainty to create a safety cushion.

Progress

Whereas the hold-back procedure involves slowing down with a view to looking, waiting and deciding on what action is required, powered progress involves proceeding after considering all the available information and deciding it's safe to go. This often includes creeping and peeping. Using first-gear clutch control, slowly edge forwards so that you can look round any obstruction, or in all directions at blind junctions, before making any commitment to proceed.

For making powered progress away from hazards, the point at which the decision to go is taken will dictate which gear to select. Remember, gears are for going – not for slowing! Select a gear that will be appropriate for the speed and power requirements.

Speed control and steering

The control skills required will depend on the need either to make powered progress or to hold back. Powered progress involves holding the car still or moving off under full control on all gradients, then making efficient progress through the gears, taking into account changing conditions and gradients. Holding back involves slowing down using either deceleration or controlled rates of braking, depending on gradients, and stopping if the need arises and securing the vehicle. Which procedure is necessary depends on the road and traffic environment.

To drive efficiently, effectively and economically you should:

- have a thorough knowledge of all the different skills involved in proper speed control;
- understand the principles of the safe use of speed in relation to acceleration, braking and cornering;
- be aware of the overall stopping distances in both good weather and poor driving conditions and have the ability to put them into practice.

Pay particular attention to signs and markings so that you are aware of the speed limit for the road you are using. You should be aware of the need to make proper progress according to the road and traffic conditions. Demonstrate that you are a confident driver – if you put on a show of being overcautious, you may inconvenience other people or put them in danger. Maintain all-round awareness by keeping a check on what is happening all around your vehicle before you make any changes to your speed or direction.

Car control

An efficient system of car control should take into account the natural and mechanical forces that affect the stability of a vehicle in motion. Your system of driving must take into consideration other road users' actions by having built-in safety margins that should help to compensate for:

- human error;
- deficient skills;
- minor lapses in concentration;
- mistakes by other road users.

Applying an efficient system should ensure that you will always have time to maintain control of your vehicle in a sympathetic manner. Points to remember are:

- The speed of your vehicle should always be such that you can stop in a controlled manner well within the distance you can see to be clear. To do this you need to look for and respond to:
  - obstructions on your intended course;
  - the potential for other road users to move into your intended course from blind areas;
  - restrictions to your sightlines caused by road features such as bends, hill crests or dips in the road;
  - obstructions that may be hidden by restricted sightlines.
- Control and speed should take into account the natural and mechanical forces that affect the stability of vehicles in motion. You should demonstrate an awareness of the:

- physical road-holding and handling limitations of your car;
- tyre and road surface adhesion;
- increased stopping distances in wet and icy conditions;
- effects of camber and gravity;
- aerodynamic forces acting on the vehicle.

- To minimize the effects of the forces that affect the stability of vehicles in motion, you should:
  - use the accelerator, brakes and steering smoothly and progressively;
  - avoid excessive acceleration or braking when negotiating bends and corners;
  - avoid changing gear when your hands would be better engaged on the steering wheel, for example when negotiating sharp bends and turns;
  - avoid unnecessary gear changes when selective changing is more appropriate;
  - keep both hands on the wheel when braking, accelerating and cornering;
  - accelerate progressively when negotiating a curved path.

If you are sympathetic to the needs of your vehicle, you will improve fuel efficiency and prolong the vehicle's working life. Try to:

- avoid unnecessary or fidgety movements on the accelerator;
- use the accelerator and footbrake early and progressively;
- avoid excessive clutch slip, drag and unnecessary coasting;
- avoid excessive tyre wear by cornering at lower speeds;
- avoid using the gears to reduce speed;
- use cruise control if it's available.

Handbrake

Use the handbrake:

- when the vehicle is stationary on up- and downhill slopes;
- if you're going to be stationary for more than a few seconds, that is, for longer than the time it would take to apply and then release it again; and of course,
- when parked.

However, if you plan ahead properly and anticipate any changing circumstances, you should be able to minimize the number of times you need to come to a complete stop. By planning and creeping slowly forwards, you are creating time for the hazard to clear, making the stop either unnecessary or minimal. For such short stops the use of the handbrake is obviously unnecessary.

Brakes and gears

When slowing down, keep both hands on the wheel and (unless you are on an uphill gradient) use the footbrake to reduce speed. After slowing down, change to a gear that is appropriate for negotiating the hazard. For example, when approaching a left turn in, say, fourth or fifth gear, brake to reduce the speed sufficiently and then change into the gear required to negotiate this particular corner. When approaching a T junction where your view of the main road is restricted, brake to slow down until the car has almost stopped, push down the clutch and release the pressure from the brake to allow the vehicle to roll slowly. Just before stopping, change into first gear, ready to go again. As well as being a waste of fuel, changing down to reduce the speed is unsympathetic and causes unnecessary wear and tear on the clutch, gearbox and transmission.

However, it is sometimes useful to use a lower gear on downhill gradients to offset the effects of gravity. In these circumstances, use the brakes initially to bring the speed under control before selecting the appropriate gear. This provides increased engine braking and reduces the risk of brake failure from overheating due to continuous use on long downhill stretches of road.

The causes and correction of skidding

Although the vehicle and road surface condition may contribute to a skid, the main cause of most skids is without any doubt the driver. There are three different types of skid and these are usually caused by:

1 excessive speed for the road conditions and/or traffic situation;
2 excessive acceleration, braking and/or cornering forces being applied to the tyres;
3 a combination of both.

The rear-wheel skid occurs when the rear wheels lose their grip. It is usually the result of excessive speed and cornering forces. Sometimes it also occurs in combination with harsh acceleration or, more usually, excessive braking. This type of skid is more easily recognized because the rear of the car slides away from the centre of the corner. If uncorrected it could cause the vehicle to turn completely round. It is essential to eliminate the cause, for example to release the accelerator and/or footbrake and compensate with the steering.

Because, in this type of skid, the driver will see that the vehicle is pointing in the wrong direction, the natural reaction will be to steer back on course.

There is a danger however, particularly with the quick response of radial tyres, for drivers to over-steer, causing the vehicle to spin the other way.

The front-wheel skid occurs when the front wheels lose their grip, leaving the driver with no directional control. It usually occurs because of turning sharply into a corner or bend at excessive speed and/or under hard acceleration or braking. It can be recognized when the vehicle fails to go in the direction in which it is being steered.

To correct the skid, the cause must be eliminated and steering control regained by momentarily straightening the wheels and/or reducing pressure on the accelerator or brake.

The four-wheel skid occurs when all four wheels lose their grip. It is usually caused by excessive speed for the road conditions or traffic situation, resulting in uncontrolled over-braking. On a wet or slippery surface the driver may even feel that the speed is increasing. Steering control is lost and the vehicle may turn broadside. The control can be partially restored by momentarily releasing the brake to allow the wheels to start turning again and then quickly reapplying the brake in a rapid on–off action. Many new cars are fitted with an anti-lock braking system that will work in the same way, allowing the driver to regain control much more easily.

The prevention of skids is better than the cure! It is important to recognize danger signs early and act on them. For example, slowing down early when you see a group of children playing near the road will mean less braking pressure would be needed if one of them dashes out. Concentration, planning and the early anticipation of the possible actions of others is essential.

In snow and ice, slow down early with light braking pressure. Gentle braking is less likely to cause skidding than changing into a lower gear. Use gradual acceleration and keep in the highest gear possible without distressing the engine. When going uphill in snow, try to maintain a steady momentum by staying well back from the vehicle ahead.

Drive at safe speeds for the road-surface conditions. Accelerate, brake and corner gently. Drive more slowly on wet, icy and slippery surfaces. Watch out for loose gravel, fallen leaves and damp patches under trees. Make sure your tyres are correctly inflated and that they have a minimum of 2 mm of tread all around. Never mix cross-ply and radial tyres on the same axle. If you must use a mix of tyres, fit the cross-ply to the front and the radials to the rear axle.

Keep off soft verges! Read the surface conditions and slow down well before reaching any bumpy parts and speed humps. Avoid heavy braking on loose gravel and muddy surfaces and when driving through damp patches under trees.

The combination of oil, rubber dust and water can make the surface very slippery after a light summer shower following a long dry spell. In freezing temperatures, remember that black ice forms on exposed bridges first.

Emergency braking

You need to be realistic about the distance it can take to stop, particularly in wet conditions. When you have to brake quickly:

- Pivot promptly from accelerator to brake.
- Apply the brake progressively and firmly.
- Keep both hands on the wheel to keep the vehicle on a straight course.
- Apply maximum braking force just before the wheels lock up.
- Avoid braking so hard that the wheels lock up, as this will considerably lengthen the stopping distance.

If the wheels lock up, particularly in wet, slippery conditions, the brake should be released momentarily to allow the tyres to regain their grip and then quickly reapplied. This method of rapid on–off braking should not be used if the car is fitted with ABS, when pressure on the pedal should be maintained.

Whenever you are driving, you need to:

- exercise self-discipline;
- concentrate all the time and read the road well ahead;
- drive at speeds at which you can stop safely within the distance you can see is clear;
- anticipate actual and potential hazards;
- be courteous, patient and considerate;
- apply the controls gradually and smoothly;
- drive in a safe, sympathetic, effective and economical manner.

Trainee licence

06

Licence to instruct (trainee licence)

Once you have passed the ADI Part 2 exam you can, if you wish, apply for a trainee licence. This gives you the opportunity to work under supervision with fee-paying pupils and gain valuable instructing experience while you prepare for the practical instructional ability exam.

It is not essential – or a legal requirement – to take out a trainee licence; you can simply continue with your training and then take the Part 3 exam in order to be a fully qualified ADI.

You should consider some of the benefits and disadvantages of the trainee licence. On the one hand you can earn some income by working with customers who are paying you to instruct, and obtain work experience to supplement your training. On the other hand, there are costs and responsibilities attached to taking out a licence. For example, the cost of a six-month licence is currently £140 (January 2012). You will also need to undertake a complete programme of training and supervision during the period of the licence and there will, inevitably, be a cost involved.

Application

At the conclusion of your Part 2 exam the examiner will give you the trainee licence application form (ADI 3L). Alternatively, you can download the form from the Department for Transport website.

The application can be processed online. However, you will also need to complete and submit a declaration form (ADI 3L (MD)) to accompany your online application. The form has to be signed by the manager or owner of your nominated driving school or establishment.

The forms can be downloaded from www.businesslink.gov.uk or by contacting the DSA on 0300 200 1122.

When you send your completed ADI 3L form to apply for your trainee licence, you should also enclose:

- the current fee;
- a recent passport-style photograph;
- a completed ADI 21T form.

Only one licence will normally be granted and it will be at the Registrar's discretion as to whether a second may be issued.

To qualify for a licence to instruct you must:

- have passed Parts 1 and 2 of the qualifying examination;
- have undergone 40 hours of training with a qualified ADI;
- be sponsored by an ADI.

You must also:

- be eligible to take the ADI Part 3 test – the licence will be revoked if you are unsuccessful three times;
- not have exceeded the two-year qualification period starting from the date you passed the theory test.

Trainee licences are granted under the following conditions:

- You are only authorized to give instruction for the school whose address is shown on the licence.
- For every trainee licence holder there must be at least one ADI working from the sponsor's address.
- You must receive 40 hours' practical training from an ADI. This period of training must start no earlier than six months before, and be completed by, the date of issue of the licence. You must receive training in all of the following subjects:
  - explaining the controls of the vehicle, including use of the dual controls;
  - moving off and making normal stops;
  - reversing into openings to the left and the right;
  - turning the car around using forward and reverse gears;
  - parking close to the kerb, using forward and reverse gears;
  - using the mirrors and making emergency stops;
  - approaching and turning corners;
  - judging speed and making normal progress;
  - road positioning;
  - dealing with junctions and crossroads;
  - dealing with pedestrian crossings;
  - meeting, crossing the path of, overtaking and allowing adequate clearance for other vehicles and anticipating other road users;
  - giving correct signals;

- understanding traffic signs, including road markings and traffic lights;
- method, clarity, adequacy and correctness of instruction;
- the general manner of the driving instructor;
- manner, patience and tact in dealing with pupils;
- ability to inspire confidence in pupils.
- You must not advertise yourself as if you were a fully qualified instructor.
- You must abide by one of the following conditions:
  - Your sponsoring ADI must supervise 20 per cent of all the lessons you give. A record of all lessons given, along with the supervision received, must be kept on form ADI 21S. Both you and your sponsor must sign this form, which must then be returned to the DSA as soon as the licence expires.
  - Alternatively a minimum additional 20 hours' training covering all of the above topics must be undertaken. This extra training must take place within the first three months of the issue of the licence or before taking a first attempt at Part 3, whichever is the sooner. (A record of this training must be kept on form ADI 21AT and must be sent to the DSA before the end of the three-month period, or presented to the examiner who conducts the Part 3 test, whichever is the earlier.)
  - At least 25 per cent of the period of training has to be practically based and in a car at a maximum instructor-to-trainee ratio of no more than two trainees to one ADI.
  - If the training option is selected and you subsequently fail either the first or second Part 3 test, a further five hours' training must be taken before you are allowed to take another test. A declaration signed by you and your sponsor has to be provided to the examiner on the day of the test. Failure to do this will result in the test being cancelled.

If you are working under the Trainee Licence Scheme, have signed for the training option, and are attending for your first attempt at Part 3 within the first three months of the licence, you will have to produce your ADI 21T form. Both you and your trainer should sign this form to confirm you have had a minimum of 20 hours' extra training. This is in addition to the 40 hours' training required to obtain the licence.

If you have to take the test for a second or third time, you will need to provide a declaration, signed by you and your trainer, to confirm that a minimum additional five hours' training has been received. If you fail to produce any of the training declarations your test will be cancelled and you will lose the fee.

Displaying the trainee licence

Whenever you are giving driving lessons under this scheme, you must display the licence in the left-hand side of the car's windscreen. If requested by a police officer or any person authorized by the Secretary of State, you must produce the licence. Failure to do this is an offence.

Licence

If you change driving schools or your supervising ADI, you must complete a new application form (ADI 3L) and send it to the DSA together with a passport-style photo. There is no fee for this. The DSA will then issue you with a new licence showing the revised details.

If your licence is stolen you should inform the police, who should issue you with a crime reference number. To obtain a replacement licence, write to the DSA sending a passport-style photo and the crime reference number to Instructor Services and Registration Team, DSA, The Axis Building, 112 Upper Parliament Street, Nottingham NG1 6LP.

If you lose your licence, or if you are unable to produce a crime reference number, you will have to pay the current fee for a replacement licence.

The ADI Registrar can revoke your trainee licence before it expires if:

- any of the conditions under which the licence was granted are not kept;
- the licence was issued by mistake or gained by fraud;
- you have failed three attempts at the Part 3 – 'Ability to instruct' – ADI exam.

If you are not using the licence for any reason, you should return it to the Driving Standards Agency (DSA). Although you will not receive a refund for lost training time, the DSA will know that you have not had full use of the licence and this will be a factor in deciding whether to issue a subsequent licence.

Northern Ireland

The rules regarding the trainee licence in Northern Ireland are slightly different.

Trainee licences are valid for six months, and apart from very exceptional circumstances you will only be granted two licences, irrespective of the number of times you re-enter the qualifying process. It is not essential for you to hold a trainee licence before you become registered and the licence is not an alternative to registration.

Application

Application forms are available from:

Register of Approved Driving Instructors
Balmoral Road
BELFAST
BT12 6QL

To apply for a trainee licence you must:

- currently hold a full Northern Ireland, Great Britain or Community car driving licence;
- have held one of the above or a foreign licence for a total of four years out of the past six years preceding the date of your application;
- not have been under disqualification from driving for more than 12 months for any part of the four years preceding the date of your application;
- be a fit and proper person;
- have passed Parts 1 and 2 of the Register Qualifying Examination and not failed Part 3 on three occasions.

Trainee Licence Application Form – £120.00 fee (January 2012).

Licence conditions

You are only authorized to give instruction from the address shown on the licence. If you change your supervising ADI you must apply to have your licence reissued.

A Trainee Licence does not allow you to set up in business on your own behalf. You should not advertise yourself, your telephone number or any 'brand' which is unique to you, which might imply that you are an ADI.

For the six months that your licence is in force, you must be under the direct personal supervision of an ADI for at least 20 per cent of the time for which you give paid instruction; 'direct personal supervision' means that the ADI must accompany you during the lessons you give in order to monitor closely the quality of your instruction.

You must keep a daily record of the time you spend giving instruction and the supervision you receive during the first six months. This must be signed by both you and the supervising ADI. The record must be produced, on demand, to an authorized officer of the Department, and at the expiry of the licence it must be returned to DVA. Remember it is vital that you get the training and supervision mentioned above from your driving school or supervisor. It could be the difference between you passing or failing the Register Qualifying Examination or having your licence revoked.

Regulation 19(2)(a) of the Motor Cars (Driving Instruction) Regulations (Northern Ireland) 2004 states that 'where a person applies for a new licence in substitution for a licence held by him and current at the date of application, the previous licence shall not expire until the commencement of the new licence'. Therefore, if it is your intention to apply for a second licence, you must submit your application before the expiry of your first licence in order to remain entitled to give instruction for payment or reward. Failure to do so may result in your application being refused.

The use of the licence is your own responsibility. No refunds will be given for any period when the licence is not used, or for any period after you have passed the Register Qualifying Examination.

DVA recommend that anyone taking training to pass the qualifying examinations, should make appropriate checks regarding the competence of the trainer or training school which they have chosen – particularly before handing over advance fees for tuition. ADI trainers are not regulated and the Agency cannot recommend any. It is therefore in your interests to make sure that you know what to expect for your tuition fees in advance and it might be worth your while to 'shop around'. Ideally, training should cover the items listed below.

Licence advice

If your licence is lost or stolen you should report it to the police and DVA ADI Section.

The Registrar can revoke your licence if:

- any of the conditions under which the licence was granted are not kept; or
- the licence was issued by mistake or gained by fraud.

Displaying the trainee licence

It is not a requirement to display your trainee licence but it would be a good idea for you to do so to indicate to learners and to the enforcement agencies that you are permitted to instruct for reward.

Programme of training for licensed trainee driving instructors

1   Explaining the controls of the vehicle, including the use of dual controls
2   Moving off
3   Making normal stops
4   Reversing, and while doing so entering limited openings to the right or to the left

5 Turning to face the opposite direction, using forward and reverse gears

6 Parking close to the kerb, using forward and reverse gears

7 Using mirrors and explaining how to make an emergency stop

8 Approaching and turning corners

9 Judging speed, and making normal progress

10 Road positioning

11 Dealing with road junctions

12 Dealing with cross roads

13 Dealing with pedestrian crossings

14 Meeting, crossing the path of, overtaking and allowing adequate clearance for, other vehicles and other road users

15 Giving correct signals

16 Comprehensive knowledge of traffic signs, including road markings and traffic control signals

17 Method, clarity, adequacy and correctness of instruction

18 General manner

Your trainee licence shows the name and address of your training establishment. You can only give instruction from there. You are not allowed to work independently of your supervisor, eg by setting up your own school.

You must receive the required amount of supervision or additional training while your licence is still valid.

You must be a 'fit and proper' person.

Requirements for further training once you have received your trainee licence

You must receive supervision or further training from your school after you have been issued with a trainee licence to give driving instruction.

When you complete and send the ADI 21T form to the Driving Standards Agency (DSA) to apply for your trainee licence, you will have two options to choose from.

You cannot change your option once your application has been received, so you should consider which one will be best suited to you.

Option 1

Your sponsoring Approved Driving Instructor (ADI) will supervise you for 20 per cent of all lessons you give.

A record must be kept on the Licensed Trainee Supervision Record – form ADI 21S – which will be issued with the trainee licence.

You can download form ADI 21S – licensed trainee supervision record – from the Department for Transport website.

This must be signed by both you and your ADI and returned to the DSA when the licence expires.

Option 2

You will complete a minimum of 20 hours' additional training in the topics in the training programme.

This extra training must take place within the first three months of the licence or before you take your first attempt at Part 3, whichever is sooner.

The training must be recorded on the Instructor Training Declaration form ADI 21AT, which will be issued with the trainee licence.

The completed ADI 21AT form must be sent to DSA before the end of the three-month period, or presented to the examiner who carries out your ADI Part 3 test, whichever is sooner.

At least 25 per cent of the training must be practical in-car training, with usually no more than two trainees to one ADI. If you fail your first or second attempt at the ADI Part 3 test, you must provide evidence that you have taken five hours' additional training at the time of your next attempt, otherwise your trainee licence may be revoked.

The syllabus has been designed to make sure you have received the assistance you need in order to pass the ADI Part 3 test.

You should not sign the declaration on the form unless you have had the training or supervision described above.

Licence renewal

Your trainee licence is valid for six months. Further licences are issued only in exceptional circumstances, such as a long-term illness preventing you from making use of the licence.

As long as you make a valid application before your first licence expires, your first licence will remain in force while a decision on a further licence is made.

The Registrar considers each application for a further trainee licence on its merits. The Registrar is unlikely to agree to issue a new licence just to give you further time to pass the ADI Part 3 test.

If you are not granted a new licence, you have the right of appeal.

Whether you decide to take out a trainee licence and/or continue with your training, make sure you are fully prepared, in terms of instructional ability, before considering the next stage – the ADI Part 3 exam.

Note: The Government have now (March 2012) announced their intention to abolish the Trainee Licence. This is part of the DSA's programme of Modernising Driver Training and will be the subject of consultation and a review of the regulations during the next year or so.

In the meantime, and for the forseeable future, the rules and regulations for the trainee licence will remain.

ADI Part 3 – instructional ability

07

The Part 3 exam – instructional ability

The Part 3 test is a measure of your ability to give effective instruction. In the words of the DSA, the main objectives of the test are to assess the value of the instruction you give and your ability to pass on your knowledge to your pupil.

This part of the ADI exam is generally regarded as the most difficult, and in fact the pass rate is as low as 34 per cent. However, a lot of these failures can be attributed to a lack of preparation or poor training. If you prepare yourself properly and have the appropriate amount of good quality practical training, you should be able to pass without too much difficulty. At the same time, you will need to put time and effort into your training schedule, so make sure you shop around and find the best available trainer or training organization to suit your needs.

During the test the examiner will role play the part of a pupil at different stages of instruction. The test is in two parts, each of which lasts about 30 minutes. For the first part the examiner will take the role of a pupil who is either a complete beginner or a pupil who has previously received a little training. In the second part of the test the role will be either a pupil who is about test standard or a qualified driver who is taking some refresher or development training. During each phase of the test you will be asked to give instruction on one of 12 set instructional exercises. These are detailed below.

As with the Part 2, tests are conducted at DSA centres throughout the country. The examiners are specially qualified and trained in this area of expertise. You must provide a suitable vehicle for the test – details below. Remember, you are only allowed three attempts at this part of the ADI exam, so make sure you are properly and fully prepared.

How to book

You can book online at www.direct.gov.uk or by using the application form given to you at the end of the Part 2 test. The fee for the Part 3 exam is currently (January 2012) £111. In Northern Ireland the fee is £138.

Your car

The vehicle you use for the test must conform to several DSA requirements. It must:

- be properly taxed;
- have a valid MOT certificate if required;
- be in a roadworthy, clean condition with seat belts in working order;
- be fitted with statute statutory L plates front and rear or D plates in Wales;
- be properly insured to cover the examiner as a driver;
- be a saloon car bracket or hatchback or estate car with a rigid roof;
- not be fitted with a 'space-saver' tyre.

In addition the car must have:

- manual transmission;
- right-hand drive;
- a readily adjustable driver's seat;
- a seat for a forward-facing passenger;
- head restraints for both driver and passenger:
- an interior rear-view mirror for use by the examiner sitting in the driver's seat.

Insurance

The car must be insured for any liability that the examiner may have for all third-party and damage risks and for liability to any passenger. You should not restrict the insurance to any specially named drivers, as the DSA cannot guarantee in advance the person who will be conducting the test.

Supervision

Occasionally another DSA examiner may accompany you on the test. This is to ensure that the standard of assessment and marking is as uniform as possible with all examiners. If you wish, your trainer may accompany you at your request in the back of the car.

For each phase of the exam your examiner will select a topic for you to give instruction on.

The syllabus consists of 12 set exercises:

- safety precautions on entering the car and explanation of the controls;
- moving off and making normal stops;
- driving the vehicle backwards and while doing so entering limited openings to the right or left;
- turning the vehicle round in the road to face the opposite direction using forward and reverse gears;
- parking close to the kerb using reverse gears;
- practical instruction in how to use mirrors and how to make an emergency stop;
- approaching and turning corners;
- judgement of speed and general road positioning;
- dealing with coming out onto T junctions;
- dealing with all aspects of road crossroads;
- dealing with pedestrian crossings and giving appropriate signals by using your indicator and your arm in a clear and unmistakable manner;
- meeting, crossing the path of and overtaking other vehicles including allowing enough clearance, to include following distance for other road users.

At the start of each phase the examiner will explain what is required and then take the part of a pupil.

Listen very carefully to what is being described and be ready to ask questions if you really don't understand.

When this briefing has been completed the examiner will drop into the role-play situation and will stay in role as much as possible.

Remember there are no tricks or traps in the exam. As the DSA indicate in their ADI 14:

The examiner is playing the part of the pupil; their job is to test your instructional ability. Listen carefully to questions and comments when they are in pupil role; if they suggest getting on the move, for example, ask yourself whether you are giving too much stationary instruction.

Core competencies

The DSA have identified the three core competencies which form the basis of good instruction:

- fault identification;
- fault analysis;
- remedial action.

Fault identification

To identify faults correctly, you need to always find out the cause of the driving error, rather than the effect of that error. In other words, 'What happened?' 'When did it happen?' 'How did that result in the error?' To do this effectively you need to be watching your pupil closely as well as observing the traffic situation. Watch out for faults of control, observation and procedure. Faults need to be prioritized to decide whether you need to deal with them either on the move or at an appropriate stop or indeed whether you use they are ignored for the time being because they are not relevant to the lesson.

Fault analysis

Having identified and prioritized the fault you then need to work out why it happened. Was it an isolated error? Does this pupil make this type of error regularly?

Make sure that your pupil understands what went wrong and why it happened.

Remedial action

At this stage you need to decide what can be done to avoid any unnecessary repetition of the error.

Explain to your pupil:

- what happened:
- why it happened: and
- what can be done to correct it.

Offering a verbal explanation is, of course, only part of the remedy and must be followed by an appropriate practical exercise. This should be done at the earliest opportunity while the problem is fresh in the pupil's mind.

Core competencies – an example

Your pupil allows the car to swing wide after turning left onto a main road at a give way junction.

What happened? Being in the wrong position on the main road meant that we were interfering with the flow of traffic and putting ourselves in a potentially unsafe situation.

- Why did it happen?
- Was the method or control of the steering fault?
- Was it caused by lack of observations at an early stage?
- Were we in the wrong position on approach?
- Was the speed on approach to the hazard too fast?
- Was the vehicle stopped if this was required?

How do we put it right?

- By a recap on the use of brakes and gears on approach?
- By working on better control when turning?
- By improving on all observations before and while entering the main road?

In this type of situation it is rarely a single error such as steering control which is the basic fault – it is usually related to something that went wrong early in the procedure and is often a combination of two or three faults.

Instructional techniques

Lesson planning

At the start of the lesson go over the main points from the previous one so as to establish a suitable starting point or 'baseline'. This might include asking a few relevant questions and also inviting questions from the pupil.

You and your pupil should then be able to do to establish a clear indication of the aims and objectives for the lesson. Your lesson plan should take these objectives into account. However, bear in mind that you will probably need to change your initial plan if the pupil does not respond or if they revert to previous errors. In these circumstances it would be more effective to rectify the old problems rather than persevere with the original plan for the lesson.

During the test, treat the examiner as your pupil and make sure you stay in control of the lesson. Make sure, for example, that the level of your instruction is appropriate to the level of training described and portrayed by the examiner/pupil.

Because of the limitations of the exam procedure, you should tailor your instruction to suit the time available, which is about 30 minutes for each phase. In particular, keep to a minimum the amount of briefing and instruction while stationary so as to allow plenty of time for the practical instruction.

Key subject areas

In order to standardize the examiner's marking, the DSA have itemized several key subject areas which you will need to be aware of in order to prepare for the exam:

- Core competencies:
  - includes identifying analysing and remedying the pupil's faults as described above.
- Instructional techniques:
  - level of instruction;
  - planning;
  - control of the lesson;
  - communication;
  - question-and-answer technique;
  - feedback and encouragement;
  - instructor's use of controls.
- Instructor's characteristics:
  - including attitude and approach to pupil.

When you formulate your lesson plan make sure that you are pitching the level of instruction to match the ability of your pupil. If you expect too much of your pupil you will not achieve the planned objectives and may destroy the pupil's confidence. Similarly, using routes that are unnecessarily complicated and beyond the pupil's capabilities. On the other hand, if you pitch the level of instruction at a lower standard your pupil will not be stretched and will probably not make the expected progress.

Make sure that your pupil has a clear understanding of, and some practical capability in, the basics of each element of the syllabus before attempting to move on to more advanced issues.

Remember that each lesson must include a beginning, a middle and an end.

Your initial introduction should include 'why', 'when', 'where' and 'how', but should not be excessively long – a few minutes is usually enough.

The main part of the lesson will include an appropriate mix of theory and practical.

At the end of the lesson you should recap on the main points which have been covered.

Control of the lesson

To control the lesson effectively you will need to allocate an appropriate amount of time for each of the various training activities:

- theory;
- demonstration;
- practice.

This will normally be accomplished by using a mixture of different teaching methods as required for each of the different situations, including the proportion and amount of instruction on the move and while stationary. Within this overall control, however, you need to demonstrate the ability and skill to prioritize; and to respond to the changing circumstances during the lesson.

Part of the skill for you is to make your pupil feel that they are in control of the driving task, while at the same time ensuring that you are actually in control of the overall learning situation.

Communication

The examiner will expect you to use straightforward terminology without the use of unnecessary jargon. If any jargon is necessary you should give the pupil an explanation when you use that particular expression for the first time. Make sure that you give praise where appropriate and constructive criticism where it is required. Avoid the temptation to over-praise or to use exaggerated language such as 'fantastic', 'mega', 'brilliant', but encourage and motivate your pupil whenever possible.

Question and answer

You should include question-and-answer routines as part of your normal instructional methods. This is a useful way of involving your pupil in the learning process as well as a way of retaining their interest and ensuring that their attention does not wander. It is also the main method of obtaining feedback on whether they have absorbed the topic and checking that they have a full understanding of what has been learnt.

Different types of questions should be used at different times in the learning process:

- Questions at the start of the lesson should cover topics which are being dealt with on the previous lesson or any apparent areas of doubt.
- Questions during the lesson should enable you to determine whether the pupil has fully understood the subject. The answers will then often lead to further questions.
- Questions on the move should be restricted to the immediate driving task. For example – *What is happening ahead? What is the next potential hazard? What could you have done to avoid that situation?*
- Questions at the end of the lesson should simply reinforce your summary of what has happened during the lesson and should be

designed to give you and your pupil valuable feedback on progress and understanding.

- Questions from the pupil should be encouraged. Let them know from the outset that you expect questions and make sure that you leave pauses in your instruction and comments so as to allow time and space for their questions. These questions from the pupil need to be answered accurately and simply, although there will be times when you may decide to deflect the question back to the pupil by asking them to discover the correct answer. Alternatively there will be occasions when you might answer a question with another question.

Feedback

Pupils need to know when they have done well or if have made better progress than they expected. Equally, they expect to be informed when errors occur. This can be done with positive feedback, which may take the form of:

- praise for an improvement in performance;
- confirmation of a task successfully completed;
- reinforcement of an individual achievement; or
- encouragement for a particular effort.

Feedback from the pupil will show not only in the spoken word, but also:

- with body language;
- in facial expressions;
- in the practical driving.

Be ready to react to all or any of these and to respond positively with advice or guidance.

Encouragement

Your pupil should be given encouragement when needed and praise where it is due. These factors are just as important as the correction of errors. By giving the right amount of encouragement at appropriate times you will develop the pupil's confidence, which in turn will motivate them to further effort. Clearly the level of encouragement given will depend on the stage of ability of your pupil. In the early stages of learning you might give extra praise or encouragement, whereas at a later stage such praise might be inappropriate because your expectations and those of your pupil would be greater.

Use of controls

Depending on the pupil's level of ability you will probably only need to use any of the controls for demonstration purposes or to avoid a potentially dangerous situation developing. There might be times when it would be helpful to the learning process for you to assist with some of the minor controls such as wipers, washes or lights, but these occasions should be kept to a minimum. If not, your pupil could be distracted and may also develop a false sense of security.

There will, of course, be times when a minor correction to the steering or assistance with the gear lever will be advantageous, but any intervention by you should be used sparingly and with the minimum amount of interruption to the pupil's overall control of the car. If the lesson is under your efficient control there will be little need for you to use the controls.

Dual controls

The dual foot brake and clutch are useful instructional tools if used effectively. They can be used in the early stages of learning and in emergencies, but should only be used when necessary.

To avoid the overuse of dual controls, try to anticipate how the pupil is likely to react in different traffic situations. You should then be able to retain overall control of the lesson by verbal instructions and guidance without the need for the use of the dual controls. If you do need to use them, make sure that your pupil knows and understands why it was necessary for you to intervene.

You will need to consider using the dual controls if you feel that there is a potential risk of:

- injury or damage;
- a traffic offence being committed;
- excessive stress being placed on the pupil;
- mechanical damage to the car.

Your physical intervention in this way should be restricted to those occasions when the pupil has not responded, has responded incorrectly, or when there's been insufficient time.

In the early stages of learning you can, of course, use the duals as a means of helping your pupil to deal with complex driving tasks which are new to them:

- covering the clutch if you are doubtful about your pupil's ability to control the car when moving off at an exceptionally busy junction;
- using the clutch to assist the pupil and controlling the car when reversing for the first time;

- using the dual brake to demonstrate controlled braking to stop smoothly at a given position.

Continual, excessive or unnecessary use of the dual controls can be unnerving and unsettling for the pupil and can lead to a loss of faith. Using the dual controls sparingly and effectively can help to avoid that type of situation arising.

Recap

A recap at the end of the lesson is invaluable for emphasizing the more important points of learning from the main part of the lesson. The pupil can be reminded of any areas of weakness and an indication may be given on whether the lesson objectives have been achieved. You may include any points which might be appropriate for practice between lessons if that's applicable and an indication of any home study which might be required.

Phases 1 and 2

Each phase of the exam lasts about half an hour.

Listen carefully to the examiner's description of the pupil and be ready to ask questions to confirm the pupil's previous experience in the subject.

For the first phase the examiner role plays a pupil with no or little experience.

For most subjects and for most 'pupil' descriptions you will need to give a full explanation but don't spend more than a few minutes on stationary instruction. Use the rest of the available time on practical instruction, giving the pupil the opportunity to practise. Your initial briefing on the subject can usually be given at the start of the phase, but for the manoeuvring exercises you might need to do this when you get to the area where you will be carrying out the manoeuvre. In this phase, although you will be giving full instructions, don't over-instruct – reduce the amount of instruction according to the pupil's progress and ability.

In Phase 2 the examiner will explain that the pupil has some experience of the subject but that there may be a problem with one particular aspect. With some other subjects such as some of the more advanced topics the briefing will indicate that the pupil needs some instruction on this particular subject. Again, listen carefully to the examiner's description; ask a few appropriate questions to confirm the pupil's previous experience, but then get the car moving as soon as possible. You should then quickly appreciate what is needed from the way the pupil is driving. Focus your attention on the subject matter, but be ready for any other important driving faults that crop up.

For each of the two phases the examiner will select the subject from the subjects shown on page 122. Some of the exercises are only used in Phase 1, some in Phase 2 only, while others can be in either phase.

Note that in some of the exercises two completely separate subjects are included. Make sure that you treat them independently, but with the appropriate link where possible.

Example briefings

Phase 1

'I have already had one lesson with another instructor. We dealt with the controls of the car and the safety precautions, but we didn't have time for moving off and stopping.'

'My regular instructor is off sick. His car is the same as this one. We got to the point where he was going to teach me the left reverse.'

Phase 2

'My regular instructor is away, but she has indicated that I need more instruction on my judgement of speed and general road positioning.'

'I failed my test last week. The examiner marked "reverse park" on the report sheet and I'm having difficulty with this manoeuvre.'

Safety precautions on entering the car and explanation of the controls

Your examiner will play the part of someone with no previous experience. However, remember that almost without exception everyone has been in a car. For example, if the examiner's pen picture of the pupil indicates that they have worked in a garage, you will need to amend your description of the main controls; or if the briefing mentions previous experience on a motorbike, then you can use this background information to organize an appropriate lesson plan. Try to keep the pupil involved by using your question-and-answer technique and relating to what the pupil may already know.

You will be given a brief description of the pupil's experience and background and the examiner will then take on the role of a pupil. You must respond and immediately take on the role of the instructor.

Examiner's briefing

At the start of the test the examiner will normally set the scene by giving an indication of the pupil that they are going to portray and an overview of what is going to happen during this part of the exam. For example:

'This is the test of your ability as an instructor. I'm going to ask you to give instruction regarding me as your pupil, so that you can teach me in the same way that you would do normally. From time to time it may be necessary for me to instruct you. This will only be because either we want to move on to another phase of the exam or time is getting short. I would like you to assume from now on that I'm your pupil, you just met me at the office and you are going to drive to the training area where you will teach me about the main controls of the vehicle, and, if there is time, about moving off and stopping.'

The briefing will normally be given to you at the test centre. This will give you the opportunity to drive the pupil to a suitable novice training area just as you would with a genuine customer.

Use this drive to get to know the pupil a little better and to confirm that they have a valid driving licence and can read and can fulfil the eyesight test; you might also check whether they have applied for a theory test.

When you reach the training area, explain to the pupil that this is where the lesson really begins. Describe the normal routine of an experienced driver when getting into the car. This includes the pre-driving safety checks and the cockpit drill.

Explain how to get safely out of the passenger seat and into the driving seat. This includes:

- the safety of opening the passenger door;
- making sure it's safe before walking into the road round the car;
- opening the driver's door to get into the driving seat; and
- making sure all of the doors are properly closed.

Pre-driving checks

Securing the car – handbrake/neutral

Explain how the extra weight in the car can affect safety and how to ensure the car is secure before starting the engine by checking that the handbrake is on and the gear lever is in neutral. Show the pupil what to do and allow them to do it.

Explain the purpose and use of the head restraints.

Seat position

Explain and discuss the importance of sitting in the correct position and how comfort and the ability to reach and use all the controls properly will aid concentration, smooth handling and safety.

Seat belts

Check that the pupil understands the requirements with the seat belts including who has to wear seat belts, who is responsible for the safety of passengers and who might be exempt from wearing them.

Adjustment of mirrors

Your explanation should include a discussion about how to adjust all the mirrors correctly and an explanation about the different glass types as well as confirmation that there are some blind areas around the car.

Main controls

- Foot controls:
  - accelerator (gas): gentle and progressive use, works like a tap to increase or decrease the flow of fuel to make the engine speed up or slow down;
  - brake: gentle and progressive use, mirrors before use, brake lights;
  - clutch: how it works (in simple terms); when to use.
- Hand controls:
  - steering: hand position, hold on the wheel, how to turn/straighten, look well ahead to help steer in a straight line;
  - handbrake: how to release and reapply, how it works (rear wheels), examples of when to use;
  - gear lever: hand position, plenty of practice at gear selection, explain power-to-gear ratio: for example, first gear is the most powerful to get the car moving.

While stationary, explain about the ignition and reinforce checking that the handbrake is on and the gears are in neutral. Let the pupil get the feel of the controls by practising while stationary and explain your terminology; for example, 'Set the gas,' 'Find the biting point,' 'Cover the brake.'

Moving off and stopping

If you have time, you can continue by talking about and discussing the mirrors–signal–manoeuvre routine for moving off and stopping. Discuss in more detail about the blind area and what the pupil might be looking for in those areas. If necessary give a full talk-through for moving off and stopping. At this stage confirm and discuss safe stopping places.

At the end of the 'lesson' the examiner will say, 'Thank you, we'll break off at that point.' This will usually be because at this stage the examiner needs to allow time to move on to the second phase of the exam. They will then take a few minutes to complete the necessary paperwork before moving on to the next phase of the exam. This gives you an opportunity to gather your thoughts and prepare for the second phase of the exam.

Training notes

Moving off and making normal stops

The examiner will give a brief description of the person to be taught, together with a little background knowledge of previous experience. This will include confirmation that the pupil is familiar with the car.

For example:

'I'd like you to assume that I'm your pupil, you have met me at the office and we are going to drive to the training area where you will teach me about moving off and stopping.'

Listen very carefully to this briefing as you will need to establish the baseline for the lesson depending on whether or not the pupil has moved off and stopped before.

As with a real pupil at this level of experience you will probably need to drive to a suitable training area. To do this the examiner will give the route directions. On this part of the drive you can use your question-and-answer (Q and A) technique to find out about the pupil's previous experience. For example:

- 'How many lessons have you had? When were they?'
- 'Have you practised moving off and stopping yet?'
- 'Are you aware of any problems so far?'

As you drive along, you could give a simple commentary on your own driving and how you are applying the basic routines.

When you arrive at the training area use Q and A to confirm the pupil's prior knowledge. For example:

- 'Where should you look before you open the driver's door?'
- 'Why do we need to check along the left-hand side of the car before opening the door?'
- 'How might it affect your driving if you sit too close to, or too far from, the controls?'

You should be able to get some feedback on what the pupil knows about the safety precautions by giving the pupil some stationary practice. This should confirm to you the level of talk-through instruction that will be needed.

Mirrors–signals–manoeuvre routine – why and when it is used and how you will be teaching the pupil to apply for moving off, when driving along and for stopping.

Mirrors – use Q and A to establish what the pupil understands about the different types of glass and which mirror gives a true image. The next part of the discussion will depend on what the pupil already knows.

When preparing to move off, use of the mirrors should be combined with a check of the road ahead and to the sides. Explain that the mirrors do not cover all areas and the blind areas must be checked prior to moving off to look for other road users. So that the pupil understands about the blind areas, particularly on the right, point out some objects cannot be seen in the mirrors such as lampposts or gateposts. You could relate this to side roads and entrances in the area and emphasize that cyclists or pedestrians could be crossing the road diagonally or emerging from driveways. You can also use the example of an approaching vehicle and show how it disappears into the blind spot momentarily.

Signals – discuss with the pupil about how signals should be used and when they should be used. This should include the timing of signals and whether a signal would benefit another road user.

Manoeuvre – explain that this means any change in speed or direction. This will include driving the car away from a stationary position and getting into a normal driving position on the road.

For stopping, you could confirm that the MSM procedure will be applied in the following sequence:

- Use the mirrors to check on what is happening behind and how any following driver might be affected.
- Decide on whether a signal might be needed.
- Bring the car to a standstill on the left near to the kerb.

Give the pupil plenty of opportunity to ask questions and be prepared to answer any questions before you get the pupil to move the car away.

Practical instruction

Give the pupil plenty of opportunity to move off and stop in different circumstances, getting them to recognize how the procedures are adapted. For example:

- on the level (handbrake off before clutch bites);
- uphill (more care with the gas/clutch);
- downhill (foot brake applied, handbrake released, clutch up to just below bite).

Instruct the pupil through moving off and stopping a few times to build up their confidence. Continue the lesson by teaching them to move off, build up speed and change up through the gears. Encourage them to listen to the changing sound of the engine and confirm that after a bit of practice this should indicate to them when to change gear.

Make sure you cover stopping in each gear before introducing slowing-down and changing-down exercises, otherwise the pupil may think it is always necessary to change down before stopping.

Encourage regular checks of the mirrors as pupil is driving along in order to develop the pupil's awareness of the following situation and how quickly this can change.

Your talk-through should be withdrawn gradually as you see the pupil's skills developing. If the pupil begins to struggle again, then be prepared to revert to full instruction as necessary.

Feedback

At the end of the lesson use Q and A to establish what the pupil has learnt during the lesson. For example:

- 'Where should you check before moving away from the side of the road?'
- 'What are you looking for?'
- 'Why is it important to check the mirrors before signalling?'
- 'What is the normal driving position?'
- 'Is there anything you are not quite sure about?'

Look forward

Confirm that on the next lesson there will be an opportunity for more practice on these exercises and that you will be dealing with how to apply the MSM routine in other situations.

Training notes

Driving the vehicle backwards and while doing so entering limited openings to the right or left

The examiner will briefly describe the pupil, giving an outline of any previous experience and confirming their familiarity with your type of car. For example:

'For the first phase I would like you to regard me as a partly trained pupil and I would like you to teach me how to carry out a left reverse. Please correct any faults in my driving on the way down to the training area. I will direct you round the route as necessary. I would like you to assume that my other instructor has gone sick. This is the car that I normally use for my lessons. Do you have any questions before we start?'

Although you will be told of the lesson topic at the test centre, it is much more effective and efficient for you to give your explanations when you arrive at the training site – that is, where you can carry out the manoeuvre.

Before you move off, set the baseline of your lesson, using Q and A to confirm the pupil's prior knowledge and understanding of the manoeuvre. For example:

- 'How many lessons have you had? When was the last one?'
- 'Are you aware of any particular problems during those lessons?'
- 'Up to now in your lessons have you carried out any manoeuvres that include reversing?'
- 'Are you happy about controlling the car at low speeds?'

Remember, these questions are only suggestions. Use your own terminology and words that you will feel comfortable with. Listen carefully to the pupil's responses. This will give you a good idea of how to start your explanations.

Explain to the pupil that, for this exercise, we need to find a safe and convenient place and that you will direct them to a suitable area.

Make sure the pupil carries out all of the pre-driving checks and can reach and control the pedals efficiency. Something as simple as an incorrect seat position can affect clutch control while manoeuvring.

During the drive to the training area, watch out for driving faults and give advice where appropriate.

Level of instruction

Remember that you are dealing with a partly trained pupil. Do not expect too high a standard of driving and make sure you give assistance and prompting wherever you feel that these are necessary. However, do not over-instruct where the pupil is responding properly to situations and is carrying out normal driving routines correctly.

Fault identification, analysis and remedial action

Your teaching and coaching skills are being assessed all of the time – watch the pupil carefully and where there are any deviations from correct procedures, point this out and give advice on how to put things right. Use Q and A where appropriate and when it will not distract the pupil from their driving.

The examiner will direct you to a suitable area for carrying out the exercise. When you recognize the most convenient site, ask the pupil to park on the left where it is safe and well before the junction.

Feedback

Before you begin on your explanation about the manoeuvre, recap on how the pupil coped with the drive and on anything that occurred which may need attention.

Give praise where correct routines were applied and make suggestions for improvement where appropriate – remembering to back up your corrective advice with reasons.

Explanation

Use your visual aid and explain each stage of the exercise. Include information on how to position the car before starting the exercise. Emphasize the need for each of the following:

- control of the speed of the car;
- steering control;
- observations – where to look, particularly when straightening up in the new road;
- how to respond to other road users.

Control – explain how the car must be controlled at a low speed in order to allow time to see how the car is responding to the steering. You can link this in with what the pupil already knows about clutch control for creeping forward at junctions.

Steering – the wheel needs to be turned and straightened up relevant to the angle of the corner.

Observations – thorough all-round checks for other road users throughout the exercise. Discuss how to respond should any other road user including pedestrians approach from any direction.

Practice

As with any new subject your instruction should be sufficiently in-depth to enable the pupil to carry out the exercise successfully.

You must be ready:

- to react to what the pupil does;
- for how the car responds;
- to give assistance to prevent any problems arising.

Remember that first-time success will go a long way in building up the pupil's confidence. Try to ensure as far as possible that this happens.

Feedback

If the pupil responds well to your instruction and carries out the exercise with reasonable success, give plenty of praise. Give the pupil an opportunity to attempt it without your help. If required, be ready to assist at any time.

If things go wrong, explain that you will talk them through the exercise again to reinforce the key points.

Key points – reversing

- Get the pupil to check for obstructions or other potential problems as they drive past the road.
- Make sure the pupil gets into a sitting position that will enable them to turn sufficiently to be able to look through the rear window, with the seat belt removed if necessary.
- Ensure that the car is stopped about half a metre from the kerb and far enough past the corner so that it can be seen in the rear-view mirror; discuss with the pupil any guideline points for when to turn the wheel.
- Instruct the pupil to pause at appropriate times to look for other road users.

Recap

After you have carried out a couple of manoeuvres, recap on:

- the main points of the exercise;
- where the pupil achieved success; and
- what needs a little more attention.

Finally, look forward to more practice on this manoeuvre on the next lesson.

Training notes

Turning the vehicle round in the road to face the opposite direction, using forward and reverse gears

The examiner will briefly describe the 'pupil', giving an outline of previous experience and confirming familiarity or type of car. For example, a typical briefing would be:

'For this part of the exam I would like you to regard me as a partly trained pupil. I'd like you to teach me the correct way to deal with the turning in the road. I will direct you on a suitable route. Please correct any faults in my driving on the way to the training area. I would like you to assume that my regular instructor has gone sick and you are taking his place. I'm familiar with this car. Do you have any questions before we start?'

First of all set a baseline for the lesson, using Q and A to confirm the pupil's prior knowledge and understanding. Make sure the pupil carries out all of the pre-driving checks and can reach and control the pedals. Something as simple as incorrect seat positioning can affect clutch control.

Your questions might include:

- 'Have you been taught any manoeuvres which include reversing?'
- 'How would you control the car at low speeds – for example, creeping forward slowly at junctions to get a better view?'

Remember, these are only suggestions. Use your own terminology and words that you feel comfortable with and which are relevant to the described 'pupil'. Listen to the pupil's responses and organize your lesson plan accordingly.

Explain that you will need to find a safe and convenient place for this exercise.

Level of instruction

On the way to the training area remember that you are dealing with a pupil who is only partly trained. Do not expect too high a standard of driving and give help and talk-through wherever you feel it is necessary. However, do not over-instruct where the pupil is responding properly to situations and carrying out the normal driving routines correctly.

Fault identification, analysis and remedial action

Watch the pupil carefully and where there are any faults or incorrect procedures point them out and give advice on how to put them right. Use your Q and A where appropriate and where it will not distract the pupil.

Make sure you give reasons for your corrections and discuss them with the pupil so that they understand exactly what is meant.

Explanation

Before you begin your explanation recap on how the pupil coped with the drive and any incidents that might have occurred. Give praise where correct routines were applied and make suggestions for improvement where appropriate.

Discuss the reasons for this exercise, using Q and A to confirm the pupil's level of understanding. For example:

- 'Why do we need to be able to do this manoeuvre?' (not always convenient or always possible to drive forward or to find an opening to reverse into)
- 'When do you think we might need to turn the car round?' (in a confined area such as a cul-de-sac or a car park)
- 'Where do you think it would not be safe to carry out this type of manoeuvre?' (busy main roads where it would interfere with traffic flow and where there are other options available such as reversing into an opening or carrying on to a roundabout)

Use visual aids and discuss each part of the exercise, depending on the level of knowledge and understanding of the pupil. Include information on control, steering and observations.

Include in your explanation the number of movements needed to carry out this manoeuvre and how this will be affected by:

- the width of the road;
- the length of the car;
- the steering lock of the car;
- how effectively the speed and steering are controlled.

Control – link in with what the pupil should already know about clutch control for creeping and peeping at junctions. Explain how the car must be controlled at a low speed in order to give maximum time for steering.

Steering – the wheel must be turned briskly, if possible to attain full lock and then turning it back at about a metre from the kerb.

Observations – all-round checks for other road users throughout the exercise. Discuss how to respond if any vehicles are approaching.

Emphasize the need to be looking in the direction they are turning the wheel, whether this is on one of the forward movements or reversing.

Practice

As with any new subject your instruction should be sufficiently in-depth to enable the pupil to carry out the exercise successfully. You must be ready to react to what the pupil does and to give assistance to prevent any problems arising.

Remember, at a first attempt the pupil can be understandably anxious. Be prepared to assist if necessary by checking that it is safe in all directions and helping the pupil deal with other road users.

Remember – success at the first attempt will go a long way towards building up the pupil's confidence. Try to ensure, as far as possible, that this happens.

Feedback

If the pupil responds well to your instruction and carries out the exercise with reasonable success, give plenty of praise. Give an opportunity to attempt it without your help. If required, be ready to assist at any time.

If things go wrong, explain that you will then talk them through the exercise again to reinforce any of the key points.

Recap

When you have carried out a couple of manoeuvres, recap on:

- the main points of the exercise;
- where the pupil achieved success;
- what needs a little more attention.

Finally, link forward to practising the exercise more on the next lesson.

Training notes

Parking close to the kerb, using reverse gears

Although this is one of the set manoeuvring exercises, it is a subject which should only be introduced when the pupil is reasonably competent. It is therefore only used as a Phase 2 subject.

Typical briefings for this manoeuvre:

'I'm having lessons with another instructor and we have dealt with various manoeuvres such as reversing and turning in the road, but I now need to be taught the reverse park exercise.'

Or:

'I failed my test last week and the examiner marked "reverse parking" on the failure sheet. Could you correct me on this and also any errors in my general driving?'

Briefing

Explain the importance of finding somewhere safe, legal and convenient to carry out this exercise. During the drive to a suitable area remember to watch for errors and make any suggestions for improvement where appropriate.

Confirm that the pupil has practised the manoeuvring exercises and understands about clutch control, proper observations and consideration for other road users.

If the pupil has no previous experience of this manoeuvre, explain and discuss each step of the exercise, using visual aids where appropriate. Bearing in mind that the pupil is fairly experienced, do not over-instruct or treat them as a novice.

Concentrate on the elements of the exercise which are new to the pupil. For instance, where to position to begin the exercise; when to start steering; how much to steer; where to look during each part of the manoeuvre; when to straighten; and where to finish the exercise.

If the pupil has some experience at this exercise, tailor your instruction and briefings accordingly. Whatever the situation, make sure you involve the pupil in any discussion.

Your explanations should include:

- mirrors–signal–manoeuvre to get into position for the exercise. This should include an explanation of how to inform other road users of your intention by using signals, brake lights, reversing lights;
- where to position;
- good coordination of clutch, accelerator and steering; keeping a check for other road users throughout the exercise; where to start steering and how much to steer; where to look during each stage of the exercise; when to start steering back;
- how far to go back to complete the exercise.

If the pupil does not understood what is required, or has any questions, you might decide to offer a demonstration. For the purposes of the exam you will usually find that the examiner will decline the offer of a demonstration. This is purely because of the time constraints of the exam.

Practice

Where the pupil has previously carried out this exercise, let them go into the exercise without your assistance. Make any corrections where necessary. This may mean getting the pupil to pause at appropriate times to make observations.

If the exercise is new to the pupil, giving some talk-through instruction may be appropriate. This will build up confidence. You should bear in mind, however, that your talk-through should be at the correct level for the pupil's ability.

As the pupil improves, be prepared to help if any difficulty is experienced. Remain alert to the all-round traffic situation. Keep a watch out for other road users, taking any appropriate action to avoid inconvenience to others.

Feedback

Give plenty of praise where the pupil has done well and make any suggestions for improvement.

Finally, look forward to more practise on this exercise on the next lesson.

Training notes

Practical instruction in how to use mirrors and how to make an emergency stop

There are two completely separate elements to this part of the exam – emergency stops and the use of mirrors.

Introduction

The examiner will describe the pupil's background and give a brief outline of previous experience. The area around the test centre is probably not a suitable place for carrying out the emergency stop, so explain that you will be driving to a suitable place and then deal with the manoeuvre.

Example briefings:

'I have had a few lessons and would now like you to give me instruction on the correct use of mirrors and also tell me about the emergency stop.'

'My regular instructor tells me that I need some corrective instruction on my use of mirrors. Also, I am not clear about the emergency stop.'

The main objectives of this exercise are:

- Mirrors:
  - general use of the mirrors;
  - blind areas;
  - the importance of rear vision;
  - the MSM routine.
- Emergency stop:
  - how to avoid having to stop quickly.
- How to stop in an emergency:
  - by reacting quickly;
  - avoiding locking the wheels;
  - correcting skids.

Use of mirrors

Before starting the drive, confirm the pupil's understanding of the subject by using Q and A. For example:

- 'How would you adjust the mirrors?'
- 'Have you adjusted them so that they can be checked without moving your head too much?'
- 'Do the mirrors cover all areas around the car?'
- 'Where should you look before you move off?'
- 'What are you looking for?'

- 'When should you use the mirrors?'
- 'What would you do if you wanted to turn right but there is someone about to overtake you?'

Fault assessment

During the drive watch carefully for any weaknesses in the use of mirrors. Points to check include:

- incorrectly adjusted mirrors resulting in exaggerated head movement;
- no blind spot checks prior to moving off;
- lack of mirror checks in normal driving;
- lack of checks to the sides when moving off in normal road situations, for example at traffic lights or pedestrian crossings;
- incorrect response to situations;
- incorrect application of the MSM routine.

As well as being alert to the all-round traffic situation, you must carefully watch the pupil to ensure that the correct routines are being applied and also that the pupil is responding correctly to different situations.

Where any errors occur, make sure that you mention them. You will usually be able to deal with most of these on the move by asking relevant questions or by prompting.

Feedback

When you reach the training area, give some feedback on the use of mirrors in relation to what occurred. Use Q and A to establish the pupil's understanding and where problems seem to persist, remember to give an explanation so that the pupil knows exactly what you mean.

Emergency stop

In your explanation of the emergency stop you can discuss the use of mirrors on a regular basis in order to keep in touch with the all-round situation. In order to avoid the need for any unplanned and harsh braking a driver should be looking and planning well ahead so they can respond early to anything that might require a change of speed

Include in your discussions the fact that there is sometimes a need to respond quickly if something totally unexpected happens, for example if a child runs into the road. Because of the need to stop quickly, there may not be time to check the mirrors. However, as regular checks will have been made previously, the driver will have an idea about the situation behind.

Explain the sequence of actions:

- Hold the steering wheel firmly – because the weight of the car will be thrown forwards.
- Quickly pivot the right foot from the accelerator onto the brake.
- Brake firmly, but progressively.
- Clutch down just before the car comes to rest (but reassure the pupil that it is more important to be able to stop in an emergency than to keep the engine running).
- After stopping, secure the car by applying the handbrake and selecting neutral.

Skidding

Advise the pupil to avoid braking too harshly, as this can lock up the wheels and cause the car to skid. Also relate the braking pressure to the road and weather conditions.

If the car skids, explain the need to:

- remove the cause of the skid by taking the foot off the brake and then reapplying the brakes as the tyres regain a grip;
- steer to straighten up the front of the car. Use of a training aid such as a model car to show what you mean.

Before moving off again, an all-round check is needed on both sides to ensure that the blind areas are clear of any other road users.

Practice

Explain the signal you will be giving when you want the pupil to stop, but that in the meantime they should just move away and drive as normal. The signal you give should be by raising your right hand and/or by tapping the dashboard, accompanied by a firm command to stop.

Allow the pupil to move off and build up speed as normal and when the speed is built up to about 20 miles an hour and when it is safe, give the signal to stop.

Don't be surprised if the examiner declines the opportunity of practice for this manoeuvre. This will only be for reasons of time constraints and/or for safety reasons.

Feedback

Your feedback will be dependent on how the pupil responds. Common faults include:

- a slow response;
- taking time to check mirrors;

- hands taken off the wheel, for example to go for the gear lever or handbrake;
- clutch down at the same time as the brakes are applied;
- unnecessarily harsh braking;
- trying to use the handbrake to assist the stop;
- lack of all-round observations prior to moving off following the stop.

Give some remedial advice where any errors occurred and allow practice to put this right.

Link forward

Confirm where anything requires further practice in relation to using the mirrors and the emergency stop, giving praise where any correct procedures were followed and progress was made and then look forward to the next lesson.

Training notes

Approaching and turning corners

This subject may be covered at either the Phase 1 or Phase 2 stage. If it is at Phase 1 there is also the difference in ability and previous knowledge to be taken into consideration when you set a baseline for your question.

Phase 1

By asking a few questions to establish the pupil's prior knowledge, you should be able to work out how much information you will need to include in your explanation. If the pupil has not turned left or right previously you will need to confirm their understanding of the MSM routine for moving off, changing course and stopping. You will then be able to add new information to this as you explain the key points for turning into side roads.

If the pupil has turned into side roads before, you could ask: 'Tell me what the procedure is for turning left.' Respond to the pupil by either giving praise if they know the correct procedure, or by adding whatever details may have been omitted. You could then ask: 'Now, can you tell me what the differences are when you're going to turn right?'

Example examiner briefing

'I'd like you to imagine that I am one of your regular pupils. I have had several lessons and I would like you to deal with approaching junctions to turn right.'

Phase 2

The pupil should have a sound knowledge although there may be a few misunderstandings in the general procedures. Ask the pupil to run through the procedures for turning left and right. Listen carefully to the pupil's answers and respond with the appropriate amount of praise and/or correction and then adjust your lesson plan accordingly. Let the pupil drive away as soon as possible to practise and to make sure all the correct routines and procedures are followed.

'I have my driving test in a couple of weeks' time and my regular instructor has said that I have a weakness with regard to approaching junctions to turn right.'

Taking these points into consideration, your explanation and discussion with the pupil should include:

- Mirrors – confirm what the mirrors are for; why they need to be checked; and how to respond.

- Signals – should normally be used for turning as there may not be a clear view into the new road; correct timing of the signal.
- Manoeuvre – position: speed (brakes); gears; looking; deciding.

Practice

The pupil's previous knowledge and practice should dictate how much verbal assistance you will need to give on the move. For example, for a pupil with no previous experience you will need to give full talk-through instruction in order to ensure, as far as possible, that success is achieved. This will help to build up the pupil's confidence. As improvement takes place, you can reduce the amount of instruction and allow the pupil to make a few decisions. If any difficulties are experienced, further help should be offered.

With a more experienced pupil, you should watch out for errors, which might include:

- coasting;
- approaching too fast;
- approaching too slowly;
- incorrect positioning;
- not looking properly or responding to the presence of a pedestrian;
- crossing approaching traffic;
- cutting right-hand corners.

Feedback

Where any errors occur you should offer guidance on the cause rather than the effect and how to correct the problem. Remember positive assistance to prevent a potentially dangerous situation arising is much better than retrospective correction. For example, if you suspect that your pupil is going to cross the path of an oncoming vehicle it is better to say: 'Wait.' This is far better than saying afterwards: 'You shouldn't have done that.'

Give praise where improvement has taken place and look forward to the next lesson.

Training notes

Judgement of speed and general road positioning

This subject is dealt with at the Phase 2 stage. The object of the exercise is to assess whether the pupil understands the importance of: driving within the law; keeping up with the traffic flow; and driving in the correct position on the road in normal driving.

Briefing and explanation

Once the examiner has set the scene and given a description of the 'pupil', you will be able to establish the pupil's current standard and knowledge by asking a few questions such as:

- 'What is the speed limit in a built-up area?'
- 'What is the stopping distance at that speed?'
- 'What normally dictates a safe speed for the road you are travelling on?'
- 'Do you know about the two-second rule? Tell me how it works.'
- 'Where should you position your car when driving in lanes?'

Remember to give praise when the pupil's answer is correct or nearly correct and give some prompting where their understanding seems a little vague.

Practice

You should treat this pupil as a reasonably competent driver. Get on the move as soon as possible and assess their performance in relation to the above topics. Remember that positive prompts to stimulate the correct response can be more useful than retrospective correction. Sometimes this may not always be possible because of the speed or sequence of events.

Offer any remedial advice as soon as possible after the event, otherwise the pupil might have forgotten the incident at a later stage.

As well as minor errors, look particularly for mistakes in the following areas:

- progress too fast – breaking the speed limits or driving too fast for the prevailing road and traffic conditions;
- unsafe attitudes towards other road users;
- progress too slow – not keeping up with the traffic flow and causing inconvenience to other road users;
- hesitancy – not emerging from junctions when it is safe to do so;
- not positioning correctly in the road or a lane – driving too far from the kerb or too close to it; straddling lane markings; not positioning early enough in lanes.

Feedback

Remember – any feedback should be positive. Do not just confirm any mistakes but explain and discuss the cause.

Give positive advice and plenty of encouragement on where improvements need to be made.

Look forward to the next lesson.

Training notes

Dealing with coming out onto T junctions

This is a subject that may be covered at either Phase 1 or Phase 2.

The examiner will describe the pupil's background and the subject to be dealt with. For example:

- Phase 1
  'I have had a few lessons during which we have turned some corners right and left. Would you now teach me about emerging onto main roads at T junctions?'

- Phase 2
  'On my test last week the examiner marked "emerging at T junctions". I would like some assistance on improving this area of my driving.'

You must establish the pupil's previous experience by asking a few questions relative to the subject in order to establish the baseline for your lesson. Confirm the pupil's understanding of the MSM routine for dealing with hazards and junctions.

Taking these points into consideration, and dealing with emerging to the left and then to the right, you should cover:

- signs and markings on the approach and at the junction, including the difference between giving way and stopping;
- MSM routine on the approach;
- position – right and left;
- speed and gears;
- observations – mention sightlines and how they affect decisions;
- pedestrians and other road users.

Practice

The pupil's previous knowledge and experience should indicate to you how much instruction you will need to give on the move. For example, a pupil with no previous experience with emerging will need full talk-through instruction in order to experience success and to build confidence. As improvement takes place, the instruction can be withdrawn bit by bit until the pupil can cope reasonably well. If the pupil has any difficulties more help should be given as and when necessary.

For a pupil with more experience, particularly at the Phase 2 stage, you should allow them to drive without any assistance unless you can see problems which need to be corrected. Watch for any errors being committed, including:

- coasting;
- lack of observations;

- emerging unsafely;
- incorrect positioning to the right or left;
- not responding correctly to pedestrians.

Feedback

Watch the pupil and offer remedial advice where necessary about the cause of any errors. Positive assistance should be given to prevent any potentially dangerous situations arising rather than retrospective instruction after you have allowed a serious mistake to be made.

As always, give praise where any improvement has taken place and look forward to the next lesson.

Training notes

Dealing with all aspects of crossroads

This subject may be covered at either the Phase 1 or Phase 2 stage. At Phase 1 there will also be a difference of ability and previous knowledge to take into account when you set a baseline for the lesson.

Phase 1 examiner's briefing – example:

'I have had a few lessons with another instructor in a car similar to this one. We have dealt with approaching junctions, but I have not had any instruction on dealing with crossroads.'

At Phase 1, ask a few questions to establish what the pupil already knows. From that you should be able to decide how much information you need to include in your briefing. If the pupil has already had practice in dealing with crossroads you could ask them to tell you what the main differences are between this type of junction and a T junction and to outline the procedures for turning left, taking the road ahead and turning right. Make sure the pupil is aware of the need for extra observations. Also discuss what the dangers are when driving through crossroads where the markings are on the side road and where there are no markings on any of the roads. Listen carefully and add any extra information as necessary. Then let the pupil drive and watch for any errors.

If the pupil indicates that they have not dealt with crossroads, you will need to confirm their understanding of the MSM routine for dealing with T junctions, then build on that knowledge by giving information that covers the key points of this new subject.

Bearing in mind that if crossroads are a completely new subject for your pupil, you should keep to some quieter side roads – it would be unrealistic to expect them to deal with, for example, traffic-light-controlled crossroads at this stage.

Use a visual aid which shows a crossroads with give-way lines on your road and also on the road opposite. Explain how the procedure for approaching to turn left, for the road ahead and to turn right is the same as usual, applying the MSM routine. However, more observations are necessary for emerging, to take into account the actions of any driver in the road opposite. Confirm where you should be looking when driving through crossroads where the markings are on the side roads and also of the danger of driving through unmarked crossroads.

Talk-through instruction may help for the first few junctions but remember that the pupil may need help and encouragement.

Phase 2 examiner's briefing – example:

'I have my test next week and my regular instructor says that I need more instruction on approaching various types of crossroads.'

The examiner's introduction will indicate whether the pupil is at about test standard or whether they have already taken and failed a test. Make sure you do not over-instruct; instead, use questions to establish whether the pupil has a thorough understanding of the subject and to find out if they really understand what is being put into practice.

If the pupil is unsure about any aspect of procedure a short explanation might be appropriate but move on to the practical element within a reasonable amount of time.

At this stage the pupil should already have a sound knowledge of the subject but there may be a few misunderstandings in the rules of general procedures. You may be required to deal with traffic-light-controlled crossroads, so ask the pupil about the procedures for turning left and right using the MSM routine. Listen carefully and respond with appropriate praise and/or corrections as necessary. Make sure the pupil understands properly about turning right at this type of junction and use a visual aid, if appropriate, to confirm what should be done.

Depending on the standard of your pupil your briefing should include:

- MSM on the approach;
- manoeuvre – position, speed, gears;
- observations;
- emerging.

Practice

Let the pupil drive as soon as possible, watching for errors.

The pupil's previous knowledge and practice should indicate to you how much verbal assistance you need to give while on the move. For example, for a pupil with no previous experience you will need to give a full talk-through in order to make sure, as far as possible, that success is achieved. This helps to build up the pupil's confidence. As improvement takes place, your instructions can be gradually withdrawn and the pupil can be allowed to make a few decisions for themselves. If any difficulties are experienced, you can introduce more help as necessary and required.

With a pupil who has more ability, you should watch out for errors including:

- coasting;
- approaching too fast;
- incorrect positioning for left or right;
- not looking properly;

- emerging unsafely;
- not responding to pedestrians;
- crossing approaching traffic;
- cutting right corners.

Feedback

Where errors occur you should offer guidance on the cause rather than the effect and how to correct the problem. Remember, positive assistance to prevent a potentially dangerous situation arising is much better than retrospective correction.

Give praise where any improvement has taken place and look forward to the next lesson.

Training notes

Dealing with pedestrian crossings and giving appropriate signals by using your indicator and your arm in a clear and unmistakable manner

These subjects may be covered at either the Phase 1 or Phase 2 stage.

Remember that this exercise is two separate subjects – 'pedestrian crossings' and 'use of signals'.

The examiner's briefings will give an indication of the pupil's level of expertise and knowledge. For example:

'I have had 25 lessons with another instructor, who has indicated that I need some corrective instruction on the use of signals. I also need instruction on pedestrian crossings, because we have not dealt with this previously. My lessons up to now have been in a car very similar to this one.'

Listen carefully to the examiner's briefing and the description of the 'pupil'. From this you may find that there is a particular situation or type of crossing that you should concentrate on during the lesson.

If you are given the subject as a Phase 1 exercise and the pupil has not dealt with it previously, you will obviously have to give information on all of the key points. If the pupil is at the trained stage (that is, on Phase 2), you must confirm by asking a few questions that the pupil understands the rules and correct procedures for dealing with both topics.

Taking all the above into consideration, your explanation or briefing should cover:

- methods of signalling, including indicators, brake lights, road position, eye contact, not using signals unnecessarily and arm signals;
- how to recognize the different types of crossings and the rules relating to them; for example: signs on approach, beacons, zigzag lines, give-way and stop lines, traffic lights – sequence and meaning, crossings with a refuge in the centre, school crossings;
- looking and planning ahead for anyone near, or on, the crossing; how pedestrians claim priority;
- MSM on approach;
- speed on approach and stopping when necessary;
- beckoning pedestrians to cross;
- overtaking on the approach.

Explanation

The depth of explanation you give on approaching and dealing with pedestrian crossings will depend on how the pupil responded to your

questions and the knowledge demonstrated. Listen very carefully so that you can set the baseline for the lesson depending on that previous knowledge.
The main principles to consider are:

- zebra crossings:
  - looking and planning ahead for signs and markings;
  - working out what any pedestrians are likely to do;
  - checking the mirrors to see what is happening behind;
  - deciding on whether a signal would be appropriate;
  - adjusting the speed so that if a stop is necessary it will be safe;
  - leaving the crossing clear in traffic queues;
  - securing the car with the handbrake;
  - waiting without beckoning or rushing any pedestrians;
  - checking all round before moving off again;
  - arm signals – you could check on the pupil's knowledge of arm signals by asking for a demonstration of them while the car is stationary.
- pelican crossings: all of the above apply with the addition of:
  - deciding to move away on flashing amber if the crossing is clear and no other pedestrian is likely to step out;
  - omitting a signal as the lights dictate what must be done.
- practical instruction:
  - during the drive, as well as looking and planning well ahead at crossings, you should be assessing how the pupil applies the MSM routine and responding to the all-round traffic situation.
- pedestrian crossings:
  - how much talk-through is required will depend on the pupil's stated previous experience. If the pupil is responding well you may only have to identify errors and correct them. However, if the pupil has no, or very little, experience of dealing with pedestrian crossings, make sure that you give sufficient talk-through instruction to develop and improve the pupil's:
    - forward planning; anticipation and reactions;
    - application of the MSM routine;
    - car control skills on the approach to the hazard;
    - safe stopping procedures;
    - awareness of the all-round situation prior to moving away.

Practice

At the Phase 1 stage, you should encourage the pupil to look and plan well ahead by giving a commentary on what is happening. Talk through a couple of crossings and stop for a debrief to check that everything has been understood. Follow this up by letting the pupil drive and make decisions for themself – if more help is required be ready to give it.

At the Phase 2 stage, you should get the pupil on the move as soon as you are satisfied that the main points are understood. If the pupil is not responding correctly, be ready to offer suggestions for improvement. Remember that it is better to prevent a potentially dangerous situation arising than to allow it to happen and then apply corrective and retrospective instruction.

Before moving away from the test centre, and also during the lesson, use Q and A to establish the pupil's existing knowledge and understanding. For example:

- signals:
    - 'When does the Highway Code say you should use signals?'
    - 'Why is it important to check your mirrors before signalling?'
    - 'Besides the indicators, what other ways are there of signalling your intentions?'
    - 'When do you think an arm signal might be helpful?'

- pedestrian crossings:
    - 'What are the two most common types of pedestrian crossing?'
    - 'What other types are there?'
    - 'What do the zigzag lines mean on the approach to crossings?'
    - 'What should you not do within those lines?'
    - 'How would you recognize a zebra crossing?'
    - 'When must you stop at a zebra crossing?'
    - 'What should you not do if there are pedestrians waiting to cross?'
    - 'What can you expect the lights to do at a pelican crossing?'
    - 'What is the sequence of the lights at a pelican crossing?'
    - 'What does flashing amber mean?'

As well as working on pedestrian crossings, remember to watch for errors in relation to the use of signals.

Feedback

It is not absolutely necessary to keep driving until the examiner asks you to stop. Although some minor corrections can normally be made on the move, if any major problems occur you should find somewhere safe to stop and give advice.

Feedback given at regular intervals will be far more effective than leaving all of your comments to the end of a long drive.

At the end of the drive, give feedback on where any improvements have taken place and where more practice is needed. Explain any errors and give advice on how improvements may be made.

Finally, look forward to the content of the next lesson.

Training notes

Meeting, crossing the path of and overtaking other vehicles, including allowing enough clearance to include following distance for other road users

You may be asked to deal with these subjects at either Phase 1 or Phase 2. Because of the time available you will not normally be asked to deal with all of them; the examiner will usually ask you to deal with only part of the complete subject.

For example, you may be asked to deal with 'meeting other traffic', 'allowing adequate clearances and anticipation', 'crossing the path of other traffic', or 'overtaking other traffic and anticipation'.

Listen carefully to the examiner's briefing so that you keep to the particular topic that has been described. Make sure that your lesson plan is based on this information, but also watch out for faults in the pupil's general driving

By asking a few relevant questions when the examiner has set the scene, you will be able to establish the ability and previous knowledge of the pupil. This will then indicate how much information you will need to include in your explanation or how much you can ask the pupil to tell you.

At this stage (on Phase 2) the pupil should be treated as an experienced learner driver. Ask a few questions relevant to the topics the examiner has nominated. Listen carefully to the pupil's response and give praise or make corrections where necessary. You will be able to learn a lot about the pupil from these responses.

If you are given acceptable information, get moving as soon as possible so as to assess the pupil's strengths and weaknesses.

Your explanation should include:

- mirrors–signal–manoeuvre;
- meeting approaching traffic – parked vehicles on your side of the road, the other side of the road and both sides of the road;
- allowing adequate clearance to parked vehicles – what to look out for;
- anticipating what to expect and what others might do in busy areas;
- crossing the path of other traffic;
- overtaking other traffic – explain how MSM is slightly different;
- keeping a safe following distance.

Practice

At Phase 1 the standard of the pupil will dictate how much talk-through or help is needed during the drive. You will get a clear indication of this from the responses to your questions and from the way the pupil is driving. Remember at this stage it is important that you build confidence in the pupil and then allow them to do things for themselves.

At Phase 2 you should treat the pupil as a more experienced learner and get on to the practical driving as soon as possible. If you can see that the pupil is not responding to what is happening or what could possibly happen, do not leave things too late and let a potentially dangerous situation develop. For example, if the pupil is not responding to someone else's indicators or brake lights you could give a prompt. You could ask: 'Have you seen the signal ahead?' 'What you think that driver is going to do?' 'What can you do?'

During the drive, watch for the pupil's errors and give correct advice where necessary. At any time, if you find that several errors are building up, get the pupil to stop in a safe position and discuss the relevant points. Don't feel you have to wait until the end of the session. During your discussions, the examiner in the role of a pupil will give a clear indication of what is required next. Listen carefully!

Errors could include:

- not applying the MSM routine correctly;
- not giving way to oncoming traffic where appropriate;
- crossing the path of other traffic unsafely;
- attempting to overtake unsafely;
- following too closely;
- not giving sufficient clearance to parked vehicles;
- not slowing down where clearances are limited;
- not anticipating the actions of other drivers, pedestrians or cyclists.

Feedback

It is important that the pupil learns something during the lesson. Where errors are committed, give advice as to how they have been corrected and explain why. This will help develop the pupil's understanding and promote positive attitudes.

Give praise where any improvement has taken place and look forward to the next lesson.

Training notes

The pre-set tests

To ensure that all candidates have a test of equal difficulty, and that there is a balance between the two phases, the 12 set exercises listed below are arranged as 'pre-set tests' (PST). Some subjects – for example, 'pedestrian crossings and signals' – are used more often than others. Where a test exercise involves several subjects, for example 'meet, cross and overtake other traffic', your examiner will give a clear indication of those subjects you are to include. Make sure that you listen carefully and structure your lesson accordingly.

The system of pre-set tests also means that you are unlikely to be given the same subjects on any subsequent retest.

Set exercises

Safety precautions on entering the car and explanation of the controls;

- moving off and making normal stops;
- driving the vehicle backwards and while so doing entering limited openings to the right or left;
- turning the vehicle round in the road to face the opposite direction, using forward and reverse gears;
- parking close to the kerb, using reverse gears;
- practical instruction in how to use mirrors and how to make an emergency stop;
- approaching and turning corners;
- judgement of speed and general road positioning;
- dealing with coming out onto T junctions;
- dealing with all aspects of crossroads;
- dealing with pedestrian crossings and giving appropriate signals by using your indicator and your arm in a clear and unmistakable manner;
- meeting, crossing the path of and overtaking other vehicles, including allowing enough clearance to include following distance for other road users.

PST pairings

PST 1:
Phase 1 – safety precautions on entering the car and explanation of the controls;
Phase 2 – dealing with all aspects of crossroads.

PST 2:
Phase 1 – moving off and making normal stops;
Phase 2 – meeting, crossing the path of and overtaking other vehicles, including allowing enough clearance to include following distance for other road users.

PST 3:
Phase 1 – turning the vehicle round in the road to face the opposite direction, using forward and reverse gears;
Phase 2 – approaching and turning corners.

PST 4:
Phase 1 – driving the vehicle backwards and while so doing entering limited openings to the right or left;
Phase 2 – dealing with coming out onto T junctions.

PST 5:
Phase 1 – practical instruction in how to use mirrors and how to make an emergency stop;
Phase 2 – judgement of speed and general road positioning.

PST 6:
Phase 1 – practical instruction in how to use mirrors and how to make an emergency stop;
Phase 2 – parking close to the kerb, using reverse gears.

PST 7:
Phase 1 – approaching and turning corners;
Phase 2 – dealing with pedestrian crossings and giving appropriate signals by using your indicator and your arm in a clear and unmistakable manner.

PST 8:
Phase 1 – dealing with coming out onto T junctions;
Phase 2 – meeting, crossing the path of and overtaking other vehicles, including allowing enough clearance to include following distance for other road users.

PST 9:
Phase 1 – dealing with all aspects of crossroads;
Phase 2 – dealing with pedestrian crossings and giving appropriate signals by using your indicator and your arm in a clear and unmistakable manner.

PST 10:
Phase 1 – meeting, crossing the path of and overtaking other vehicles, including allowing enough clearance to include following distance for other road users;
Phase 2 – judgement of speed and general road positioning.

According to the DSA, the most common contributory factors for failing the Part 3 examination are:

- a briefing that is too long, muddled or repetitive;
- expecting too high a standard from the pupil in the beginner or part-trained stage;
- not instructing at a level appropriate to the pupil's needs, for example over-instruction or under-instruction;
- inability to recommence instruction at a different point or to go back and explain again any weaknesses in one or more of the core competencies – fault identification, fault analysis or remedial action;
- treating a pupil as a beginner in the trained/full-licence-holder stage.

Ten useful tips for the Part 3 examination from the DSA

1 Ensure that you have had plenty of training and practice at giving instruction at varying levels of pupil ability. You should be able to give a lesson on any aspect of the learner-driver training syllabus. In doing so you should be more than just familiar with any of the pre-set tests that you may be asked to cover.

2 Listen carefully to the description of each pre-set test on which you will be asked to give instruction, and to the description of the 'pupil' that the examiner intends to portray. Should you have any queries about the format of the examination, ask the examiner before they go into the role of pupil.

3 Generally speaking, the beginner or partly trained pupil will need positive instruction and guidance to establish correct driving procedures, whereas the trained pupil often benefits more from thought-provoking questions. This process is often referred to as the question-and-answer technique.

4 The test consists of two half-hour phases. The length of briefings should be appropriate to the pupil's knowledge and geared to that time. This may mean that you will need to adjust your normal briefing time. Briefings should be brief and be given when appropriate. They should clearly relate to the subject matter expected to be covered.

5 Remember that you are in charge of the lesson; watch how the pupil is responding to your instruction and adjust your instruction to meet the pupil's needs.

6 It is important that you respond to pupil performance. You will be expected to correct other driving faults in addition to those included in the specific exercises.

7 It is not always necessary to stop to deal with some driving faults. Consider what will need to be the appropriate level of instruction for your pupil. Some faults can be corrected more effectively on the move.

8 Pupils will benefit from appropriate praise and encouragement.

9 There are no tricks or traps in the Part 3 examination. The examiner is playing the part of a pupil; their job is to test your instructional ability. Listen carefully to questions and comments when they are in pupil role; if they suggest 'getting on the move', for example, ask yourself whether you are giving too much stationary instruction.

10 The test of instructional ability is recognized as the most difficult of the three parts of the ADI qualifying process. It is important that you do not attempt this part of the examination until you are confident that you can give instruction on all of the pre-set tests to a satisfactory standard.

The examiner's marking sheet

The marking sheets for the PSTs are reproduced on pages 167 to 176 of *The Driving Instructor's Handbook* (17th edition).

Using these markings, the examiner will assess your overall performance on both phases. In particular, you will be assessed on your ability under the three main headings of core competencies, instructional techniques and instructor characteristics. The examiner will also mark your instructional ability on the specific subject. The maximum grade attainable in each phase is 6. The minimum level for a pass is grade 4 in each phase. However, the examiner makes an overall assessment by taking into consideration the overall markings in each section.

Criteria for grading

6 Overall performance to a very high standard with no significant instructional weaknesses.

5 A good overall standard of instruction with some minor weakness in instructional technique.

4 A competent overall performance with some minor deficiencies in instructional technique.

3 An inadequate overall performance with some deficiencies in instructional techniques.

2 A poor overall performance with numerous deficiencies in instructional techniques.

1 Overall standard of instruction extremely poor or dangerous with incorrect or even dangerous instruction.

You must remember that because of this overall assessment of what actually happens on the day, no two tests can ever be the same. Even the manoeuvre exercises cannot be rehearsed, and you will need to be able to adapt to what is happening in different circumstances. This is all part of the test of your potential to become an effective teacher of driving.

When you pass

You will be given a letter confirming the result, and you may apply for entry on to the Register of Approved Driving Instructors (Car). Complete the application form on the reverse of the letter and send it with the current fee (£300 at January 2012). This must be done within 12 months of the date you pass. Registration then becomes renewable every four years.

The fee in Northern Ireland is currently £240.

Registration declaration

When you apply for registration, you must sign a declaration to the effect that you will:

- notify the Registrar of any change of name, address or place of employment;
- notify the Registrar if convicted of any offence;
- return the certificate if your registration lapses or is revoked;
- agree to undergo, when requested by the Registrar, a check test conducted by DSA staff.

Full details of the registration process are in Chapter 8.

If you fail

If the test was your first or second attempt and you are still within the two-year period for taking the exam, you can apply for a retest. The examiner will have given you an application form for this purpose.

If you fail at three attempts, or if you are not within the two-year period, you will have to wait until the two years have elapsed and then start the three parts of the examination again. It is therefore sensible to be prepared to invest in sufficient training with an experienced tutor in preparation for this part of the exam.

Regardless of whether you pass or fail, you can obtain more details about your test by contacting the DSA. You can do this by contacting the examiner, who will be able to give advice to help with your instructional techniques. The examiners are normally available in your local area offices on a Friday.

The ADI Certificate

After passing the instructional ability part of the exam you can apply for registration as an ADI. When your application has been accepted by the DSA you will receive the official ADI Certificate of Registration. This will incorporate your name, photograph, ADI number and the date of issue and expiry of the certificate, which will be four years from the date of its issue. As a qualified instructor, whenever you are giving tuition, you must display the official green certificate on the left-hand side of the car's windscreen, and produce your certificate if requested by a police officer or any person authorized by the Secretary of State. (Failure to do so constitutes an offence.) If you can satisfy the Registrar that your certificate has been lost, damaged or destroyed, the DSA will issue a duplicate on payment of the current fee.

This chapter gives an overview of the instructional ability part of the ADI exams and how to prepare for it. Remember, however, that there is no substitute for good quality practical in-car training from someone who is qualified and experienced in this area of expertise. Reading about it in a book such as this is not enough!

ADI
Registration

08

O nce you have passed all three parts of the ADI exam you can apply for registration as an Approved Driving Instructor (ADI).

You must apply within 12 months of passing the final part of the exam.

For the application to be accepted by the DSA you must show that you are still 'a fit and proper person'.

Registration as an ADI is normally for four years.

Application

Your application can be made online or by post.

Apply online at www.businesslink.gov.uk/currentADI.

For postal applications, send the form ADI 12 to DSA at Nottingham together with the appropriate payment and an up-to-date passport-style photo. Make sure you put your ADI personal reference number on the back of the photo.

The current cost of registration at January 2012 is £300.

In Northern Ireland the fee is £240.

Registration

When your application has been accepted by the DSA you will receive the official certificate of registration. This carries your photo, your name and the personal reference number that was allocated when you first applied. You must display the certificate on the windscreen of your car whenever you are giving instruction.

You may be asked to produce the certificate at any time by a police officer or by an authorized officer of the Department for Transport.

If you lose the certificate, or if it is stolen, you should report the loss to the police as soon as possible. The DSA will normally issue a replacement document as long as they sure that the original has been lost, stolen or destroyed.

If you change your address or have any change in your personal circumstances that would affect your registration as an ADI you must notify the DSA as soon as possible.

You must inform the DSA if, for example, you:

- change your name, your home address or your business address. The DSA will then update their records so that you continue to receive notification about your check test, re-registration and so on.
- decide to stop giving instruction for any reason such as illness or living abroad.
- receive any conviction or caution, whether for motoring or non-motoring offences.

You can contact the DSA to notify them about any of the above changes by:

- telephone: 0300 200 1122;
- e-mail: ADIreg@dsa.gsi.gov.uk;
- post:

  Instructor Services and Registration Team
  DSA
  The Axis Building
  Upper Parliament St
  NOTTINGHAM
  NG1 6LP

The ADI check test

As part of your registration commitment you will be required to undergo a periodic check on your ability to instruct. The check test shows the DSA that your ability to give instruction is up to the same standard as on the ADI Part 3 exam.

Soon after you have registered as an ADI you will be seen by a senior examiner from the DSA (a 'Driver Training Assessment Manager'). Assuming that your ability to instruct is satisfactory you will be given a grade of 4, 5 or 6. If your instruction is not up to standard the examiner will allocate a grade of E. This grade stands for 'educational' and means that you will be seen again within a few months to be given a revised grading.

The check test is normally conducted by the examiner observing you on a normal driving lesson with one of your regular pupils. However, if you are not able to provide a pupil at the required time the examiner may role play the part of pupil as in the Part 3 ADI exam.

The examiner will assess your instruction and will decide whether the subjects used were:

- covered satisfactorily (or better);
- incomplete or unsatisfactory in some way;
- incorrect, dangerous or not covered.

During the check test your instructional ability is assessed in the areas shown below.

Core competencies

- fault identification:
  - identify any important weaknesses in the pupil's driving;
  - prioritizing any faults.
- fault analysis:
  - explanation to the pupil of what went wrong and why.
- remedial action:
  - teaching the pupil how to avoid committing the same fault.
- consolidation with practice.

Instructional techniques

- recap at the start of the lesson:
  - refer back to the pupil's previous lesson and what was covered.
- aims and objectives of the lesson:
  - discuss and agree the main objectives for the lesson.
- level of instruction:
  - the level of instruction should match the pupil's level of ability and experience;
  - avoid over-instructing or under-instructing.
- planning of the lesson:
  - allocate a suitable amount of time to theory and practical instruction;
  - avoid excessively long briefings or explanations.

- control of the lesson:
  - make sure you remain in control of the situation. Give instructions and directions clearly and firmly. Don't be afraid to stop the car to give instruction when appropriate.
- communication:
  - use straightforward language suitable for the individual pupil. Avoid jargon. Make sure the pupil has understood.
- question-and-answer technique:
  - use open and closed questions where appropriate. Be careful when using questions starting with 'Why …'. Use Q and A at the start of a lesson, during the lesson and at the end, but do not rely on questions alone. Give the pupil opportunities to ask questions.
- feedback and encouragement:
  - balance the amount of praise and criticism. Feedback should be positive.
- instructor's use of controls:
  - avoid using the dual controls whenever possible. If you do use them, explain why.
- recap at end:
  - recap on the lesson and look forward to the content of the next lesson.

Instructor characteristics

- attitude:
  - make sure that you are enthusiastic, encouraging and that you present a positive attitude to the pupil.
- approach to pupil:
  - maintain a friendly and approachable manner, but with a professional instructor–pupil relationship.

ADI grading

As a newly qualified ADI you can expect to be asked to attend for a check test within a few months of passing the qualifying exams. This first check test is regarded as an educational visit by the DSA and it is normal for the instructor to be allocated an E grade. However, if the examiner feels that your instruction is up to a reasonable standard despite your inexperience as an ADI, you may be allocated a grade of 4, 5 or even 6.

Once you have been given a grade you can expect to have another check test within a few months if the grade was E or in about two to four years for grades 4 to 6.

On a regular check test if the grading is below 4 it is regarded as unacceptable or inadequate and in this event the instructor would be revisited in a much shorter time.

The general public – and your prospective pupils – seem to know very little about the instructor grading system; most people assume that all instructors are qualified and that is about the limit of their interest or awareness. Even if customers are aware of the grades it seems that the general opinion is that 1 would be the top grade, when in fact it is the opposite. In view of this, if you manage to make the top grade on a check test, make sure your pupils know what it means.

Check test checklist

Looking ahead to after you have qualified as an ADI and when you take your check test (and, indeed, on regular lessons), the following checklist will ensure that you have not missed out essential items.

The car:

- fuel – have you got sufficient fuel for the extended lesson and travel?
- clean and tidy inside and out;
- seat belts (front and rear) working properly;
- tax disc (road fund licence disc) – valid?
- insurance – up to date?
- MOT – if required;
- tyres – are they legal; pressures?
- lights, indicators – are they all working; spare bulbs?
- mirrors – clean/adjustable;
- spare tyre and jack – all OK?
- windscreen washer – topped up;
- licence plates secure/visible;
- vehicle documentation.

Yourself:

- clean, tidy, fresh!
- water, mints;
- spare spectacles?
- sunglasses?

Training aids:

- driving manual;
- *The Highway Code*;

- pens, pencils, notepad;
- visual training aids/diagrams.

The ADI check test is covered in more detail in *Practical Teaching Skills for Driving Instructors*.

ADI grading

Grade 6

The instructor's overall performance is to a very high standard with no significant instructional weaknesses.

A concise and accurate recap on the previous lesson was given with realistic, attainable objectives set for the current lesson. There was dialogue, with pupil involvement.

The ADI consistently demonstrated the ability to vary/select the most appropriate instructional techniques to suit the needs, aptitude and ability of the pupil.

The instructor was quick to recognize and address all relevant driving faults and provided thoroughly sound analysis. Prompt and appropriate remedial action took place.

An appropriate route was chosen for the pupil's ability and experience and the instructor took every opportunity to develop the pupil's driving skills and awareness using the problems presented en route.

An appropriate learning environment was created to positively encourage the further development of the pupil's skills and good driving practice.

The lesson concluded with a concise recap, which was an accurate overview of the lesson.

The strengths and weaknesses in the pupil's performance were identified and discussed constructively.

Realistic and appropriate objectives were set for the next lesson.

A professional attitude and approach to the pupil were shown throughout the lesson.

Grade 5

A good overall standard of instruction was demonstrated with some minor weakness in instructional technique.

A recap on the previous lesson was given and the pupil was involved. Objectives were set.

The ADI demonstrated, with only minor weaknesses, the ability to vary/ select the most appropriate instructional techniques as necessary to suit the needs, aptitude and ability of the pupil.

All important driving faults were recognized and addressed with a sound analysis and appropriate remedial action being explained and practised.

An appropriate route was chosen for the pupil's ability and experience, and most opportunities were taken to develop the pupil's driving skills and awareness.

The ADI structured an appropriate learning environment in which the pupil could readily further develop their skills and good driving practice.

The lesson concluded with a concise recap, which was an accurate overview of the lesson.

The strengths and weaknesses in the pupil's performance were identified and discussed and the objectives for the next lesson were stated.

The instructor's attitude and approach to the pupil were good throughout the lesson.

Grade 4

The ADI demonstrated a competent overall performance with some minor deficiencies in instructional technique.

The recap was acceptable but with limited pupil involvement and objectives for the current lesson being outlined.

The instructor demonstrated an ability to select and/or vary the most appropriate instructional techniques as necessary to suit most of the needs, aptitude and ability of the pupil.

The ADI recognized and addressed the important driving faults, providing generally sound analysis and remedial action.

An acceptable route was chosen for the pupil's ability and experience, and advantage was taken of most of the opportunities to develop the pupil's driving skills and awareness using the problems presented en route.

The ADI structured a generally appropriate learning environment that provided opportunities for the pupil to develop their skills and good driving practice.

The lesson concluded with a general summary, giving an accurate overview of the lesson and the main strengths and weaknesses in the pupil's performance identified.

The ADI's attitude and approach to the pupil were acceptable throughout the lesson.

Grade 3

The ADI demonstrated an inadequate overall performance with some deficiencies in instructional technique.

The recap of the previous lesson was inadequate or sketchy.

The instructor did not properly set out or explain the objectives for the current lesson – nor was the pupil involved.

The instructor demonstrated only a limited ability to vary and/or select different instructional techniques as necessary to suit the needs, aptitude and ability of the pupil.

There was inconsistent identification, analysis and remedy of driving faults.

Some unnecessary retrospective instruction took place.

The route chosen was unsuitable for the pupil's ability and experience.

Opportunities were missed to develop the pupil's driving skills and awareness using the problems that presented themselves en route.

The ADI failed to structure a learning environment to enable the pupil to develop skills and good driving practice.

The summary at the end of the lesson was inaccurate or incomplete.

Many of the strengths and weaknesses in the pupil's performance were not identified, or were treated superficially.

There were shortcomings in the ADI's attitude and approach to the pupil.

Grade 2

The ADI demonstrated an overall poor performance with numerous deficiencies in instructional technique.

There was little or no recap given on the previous lesson and a failure to set objectives for the current lesson.

The instructor was unable to vary/select instructional techniques as necessary to suit the needs, aptitude and ability of the pupil.

Many problems occurred with the correct identification of driving faults, their analysis, and remedial action was very late.

The route chosen was unsuitable for the pupil's ability and experience and numerous opportunities were missed to develop the pupil's driving skills and awareness.

It was a poor learning environment in which the pupil would be unable to develop skills and good driving practice.

A superficial summary was given at the end of the lesson, with the main strengths and weaknesses in the pupil's performance not being mentioned.

The ADI demonstrated serious shortcomings in attitude and approach to the pupil.

Grade 1

The ADI's overall standard of instruction was extremely poor or dangerous with incorrect or even unsafe instruction.

No recap was given on the previous lesson and no objectives set for the current one.

The instructor was unable even to recognize the need to vary/select the most appropriate instructional techniques as necessary to suit the needs, aptitude and ability of the pupil.

Driving faults were not identified, analysed or corrected. Many of these were of a serious or dangerous nature.

A totally unsuitable route was chosen for the pupil's ability and experience.

The ADI failed to use the opportunities that presented themselves en route to develop the pupil's driving skills and awareness.

There was no attempt to structure any kind of learning environment.

No summary was given at the end of the lesson.

The ADI demonstrated very serious shortcomings in attitude and approach to the pupil.

At the end of the test

You will be given a verbal debriefing and handed an ADI 26 form showing the markings under the various headings. A copy of the 'working sheet' marked by the examiner during the test is available from the DSA.

Pass Plus

Pass Plus is a scheme for helping new drivers to improve their skills and knowledge soon after passing their L test. The scheme is operated by the DSA with support from insurers and the driver training industry. One of the main benefits to the pupil is the availability of discounted insurance from a range of insurers.

The programme of training builds on the pupil's skills and knowledge and helps them deal with a variety of hazards that they would not necessarily have encountered while learning to drive or on test.

Pass Plus consists of six modules:

- in all weathers;
- on rural roads;
- at night;
- on dual carriageways;
- on motorways.

To be able to offer this service to your pupils you must be an ADI and will need to register as a Pass Plus instructor with the DSA.

You can register online, by post or by phone.

Online: at www.businesslink.gov.uk.

By post: send your payment to DSA, PO Box 280, Newcastle upon Tyne, NE99 1FP.

By phone: 0115 936 6504.

As part of the registration process you will need to buy a starter pack, which includes:

- an instructor's guide;
- training report forms;
- pupil guide;
- progress reports;
- promotional leaflets;
- a list of participating insurers.

The current cost of a starter pack (at January 2012) is £37, with refill packs costing £29.

Pass Plus is available for any car driver who holds a full driving licence, but is normally suitable for someone who has held a full licence for less than 12 months.

Pass Plus usually takes about six months of training, but it can take longer if necessary. There is no test involved, but the pupil is continually assessed during each of the modules. It is a practical course and each module should, ideally, consist of a practical in-car session. However, local conditions and the time of year sometimes mean that you might need to give some modules as theory sessions. For example, if there are no motorways within reasonable distance a theory session can be given, but overall the course should be mainly practical.

At the end of the six modules you must complete a training report indicating the pupil's standard in each module. To pass the course the pupil needs to reach a satisfactory standard in all the modules.

For more information, contact the DSA Pass Plus section at: Pass Plus Team, DSA, The Axis Building, 112 Upper Parliament Street, Nottingham NG1 6LP; tel 0115 936 6504; e-mail passplus@dsa.gsi.gov.uk.

Code of Practice for ADIs

The Voluntary Code of Practice for ADIs was drawn up by the DSA in consultation with the driver training industry with the aim of raising professional standards in the industry. The DSA recommend that all instructors should agree to abide by the code when registering as an ADI.

Personal conduct

The instructor will at all times behave in a professional manner towards clients.

Clients will be treated with respect and consideration.

The instructor will try to avoid physical contact with a client except in an emergency or in the normal course of greeting.

Whilst reserving the right to decide against giving tuition, the instructor will not act in any way which contravenes legislation on discrimination.

Business dealings

The instructor will safeguard and account for any monies paid in advance by the client in respect of driving lessons, test fees or for any other purpose and will make the details available to the client on request.

The instructor on or before the first lesson should provide clients with a written copy of the instructor's terms of business, to include:

- legal identity of the school/instructor with full address and telephone number at which the instructor or their representative can be contacted;
- the price and duration of lessons;
- the price and conditions for use of a driving-school car for the practical driving test;
- the terms under which cancellation by either party may take place;
- procedure for complaints.

The instructor should check a client's entitlement to drive the vehicle and their ability to read a number plate at the statutory distance on the first lesson. When presenting a client for the practical driving test the instructor should ensure that the client has all the necessary documentation to enable the client to take the test and that the vehicle is roadworthy.

Instructors will advise clients when to apply for their theory and practical driving tests, taking account of local waiting times and forecast of the client's potential for achieving the driving test pass standard. The instructor will not cancel or rearrange a driving test without the client's agreement. In the event of the instructor's decision to withhold the use of the school car for the driving test, sufficient notice should be given to the client to avoid loss of the DSA test fee.

The instructor should at all times, to the best of their ability, endeavour to teach the client correct driving skills according to DSA's recommended syllabus.

Advertising

The advertising of driving tuition shall be honest; claims made shall be capable of verification and comply with codes of practice set down by the Advertising Standards Authority.

Advertising that refers to clients' pass rates should not be open to misinterpretation and the basis on which the calculation is made should be made clear.

Conciliation

Complaints by clients should be made in the first instance to the driving instructor/driving school/contractor following the complaints procedure issued. Failing agreement or settlement of a dispute, reference may be made to DSA's Registrar of Approved Driving Instructors who will consider the matter and advise accordingly.

Should the Registrar not be able to settle the dispute, they may set up a panel, with representatives from the ADI industry, to consider the matter further or advise that the matter should be referred to the courts or other statutory body to be determined.

Driver's record

The DSA, in consultation with the driver training industry, has produced a 'driver's record' covering the recognized syllabus for learning to drive.

By covering the structured syllabus and by completing the driver's record both you and the pupil can maintain an accurate record of progress in preparation for the practical test.

Copies can be downloaded from www.directgov.

Continuing professional development (CPD)

As a professional driver trainer you should make sure that you keep yourself up to date with current legislation, regulations and best practice in terms of instruction and business matters. To do this, the DSA recommends that all ADIs should undertake at least seven hours of CPD each year.

This can be done in different ways, including:

- updating your own skills in driving or instructing;
- attending seminars, workshops or meetings at local or national level;
- spending time developing your business skills;
- networking with groups of colleagues;
- online research.

By registering your commitment to ongoing CPD you can have your business details highlighted and promoted on the directgov website in the section 'Find your nearest instructor'. This service enables prospective pupils to make an informed choice when looking for an instructor in their local area.

Official DSA theory test answers

09

Band 1 – Road procedure

1.1 Cycles

1.2 alert others to your presence

1.3 in the right-hand lane

1.4 help other road users know what you intend to do

1.5 an open stretch of road

1.6 passing pedal cyclists

1.7 stay behind and not overtake

1.8 behind the line, then edge forward to see clearly

1.9 ignore the error and stay calm

1.10 give way to them

1.11 any vehicle

1.12 overtaking

1.13 there is a queue of traffic to your right that is moving more slowly

1.14 leave by the next exit

1.15 it allows easy location by the emergency services

1.16 gain speed on the hard shoulder before moving out onto the carriageway

1.17 on a gradient

1.18 30 mph

1.19 overtaking or turning right

1.20 continue in that lane

1.21 to build up a speed similar to traffic on the motorway

1.22 drop back further

1.23 it is more difficult to see events ahead

1.24 wait for the signal to be cancelled before overtaking

1.25 pedestrians

1.26 keep the other vehicle to your *right* and turn behind it (offside to offside)

1.27 give an arm signal

1.28 hold back until the cyclist has passed the junction

1.29 be aware that the driver's reactions may not be as fast as yours

1.30 wait for them to cross

1.31 temporarily obstructing traffic

1.32 be prepared to slow down and let them pass

1.33 in the centre of your lane

1.34 check for cycles on your left

1.35 one and a half times the length of your car

1.36 drive around them

1.37 in the centre of the lane

1.38 overtaking slower-moving vehicles on your left

1.39 overtake on the left if traffic on the right of you is in a queue moving more slowly than you are

1.40 wait in the side road until you can cross the dual carriageway in one movement

Band 2 – Traffic signs and signals, car control, pedestrians, mechanical knowledge

2.1 allow it to pull away, if it is safe to do so

2.2 cars

2.3 70 mph

2.4 stop and wait

2.5 the central reservation and the carriageway

2.6 white

2.7 green

2.8 60 mph

2.9 70 mph

2.10 prevented from turning right, only by oncoming traffic

2.11 your exit road is clear

2.12 must give way to pedestrians still on the crossing

2.13 a concealed level crossing

2.14 cyclists riding across

2.15 triangular

2.16 stop

2.17 red circles

2.18 octagonal

2.19 stop at the stop line

2.20 you must stop and wait behind the stop line

2.21 warnings

2.22 red and amber, then green

2.23 at least once a week

2.24 complete loss of braking on the footbrake

2.25 flashing amber

2.26 your vehicle has broken down and is causing an obstruction

2.27 misleading other road users

2.28 driving on a motorway to warn traffic behind of a hazard ahead

2.29 the brakes overheating

2.30 under-inflated tyres

2.31 in operation 24 hours a day

2.32 reduce harmful exhaust emissions

2.33 increase fuel consumption

2.34 your vehicle will pick up speed

2.35 the brakes overheating

2.36 reduce your control

2.37 move to the left in good time

2.38 planning well ahead

2.39 you will have less steering and braking control

2.40 slow down and prepare to stop

Band 3 – Driving test, disabilities, law

3.1 10 metres (32 feet)

3.2 unless a moving vehicle may cause you danger

3.3 two years

3.4 gears

3.5 not to use the mirrors

3.6 accelerator

3.7 14 years old

3.8 three years and who is at least 21 years of age

3.9 takes about 70 minutes and will include the same manoeuvres as the ordinary L test

3.10 for the whole time that they are on the Register

3.11 continue to reverse for some distance keeping reasonably close to the kerb

3.12 anyone aged 16 or over

3.13 driving too fast for the road and traffic conditions

3.14 braking promptly

3.15 normal pass certificate

3.16 21 (or over) and who has held a full licence for that category of vehicle for at least three years

3.17 60 mph

3.18 removed

3.19 is allowed to drive without restriction

3.20 candidate didn't use the mirrors effectively and act accordingly

3.21 front-seat passenger

3.22 may drive to and from an MOT test appointment

3.23 35 microgrammes per 100 millilitres

3.24 exempt for medical reasons

3.25 the vehicle is insured for your use

3.26 60 mph

3.27 cycle lane

3.28 1.6 mm

3.29 have a large deep cut in the side wall

3.30 insurance

3.31 when driving to an appointment at an MOT centre

3.32 visibility is seriously reduced

3.33 visibility is seriously reduced

3.34 are passing a road maintenance vehicle that is travelling at less than 10 mph

3.35 30 mph

3.36 it can be fitted with dual controls provided no dual accelerator is fitted

3.37 during any manoeuvre that involves reversing

3.38 have valid motor insurance

3.39 only those faults that are of sufficient significance

3.40 three years

Band 4 – Publications, instructional techniques

4.1 consolidation of the skill by means of practice

4.2 effectively over both shoulders

4.3 the rear wheels cut in when turning left

4.4 understanding of subject matter

4.5 the appropriate gear for the slope

4.6 vary the methods of instruction being used

4.7 a temporary halt in the learning process

4.8 explain what can happen as aresult of speed

4.9 associations are made with previously acquired skills and knowledge

4.10 decrease

4.11 persuasion and example

4.12 psychomotor

4.13 vary the method to suit the individual pupil

4.14 DVLA Medical Branch

4.15 used as a teaching point

4.16 memorizing facts and figures

4.17 grading the tuition in short progressive steps with attainable goals

4.18 the level at which instruction should begin

4.19 will know exactly what is expected of them and can evaluate their own progress

4.20 destroy the pupil's confidence

4.21 cognitive

4.22 position–speed–look

4.23 want to learn

4.24 to check that there is no one in the blind spot

4.25 sustained interest from the pupil

4.26 they meet the needs and ability of the pupil

4.27 attitudes to road procedures

4.28 constructively for maximum impact

4.29 memorizing facts and figures

4.30 the interpretation of necessary information

4.31 not drive yourself

4.32 check the label to see if the medicine will affect your driving

4.33 share a car when possible

4.34 pull over at a safe place to rest

4.35 etching the car number on the windows

4.36 lock it and remove the key

4.37 lock them out of sight

4.38 do little to build the pupil's faith in the instructor

4.39 tinted

4.40 reduces your concentration

Mock theory test

10

These questions are designed to test your knowledge of the syllabus for the ADI Part 1 exam.

They are not actual DSA official practice questions, but they are very similar in content and are taken from all parts of the syllabus.

Although the questions are not in any particular order, they cover the complete syllabus, with a balance of questions in each.

Band 1:

- Road procedure – 25 questions.

Band 2:

- Traffic signs and signals – 5 questions.
- Car control – 10 questions.
- Pedestrians – 5 questions.
- Mechanical knowledge – 5 questions.

Band 3:

- Driving tests – 10 questions.
- Disabilities – 5 questions.
- Law – 10 questions.

Band 4:

- Publications – 10 questions.
- Instructional techniques – 15 questions.

Remember that you need to achieve 80 per cent in each band as well as the overall pass mark of 85 per cent.

This means that you need to have 85 correct answers, with at least 20 correct in each band.

You should be able to complete the test in about 90 minutes.
Mark one answer unless otherwise indicated.

1   At traffic lights, amber means:

a) Keep going if it's safe to do so.
b) Stop under any circumstances.
c) Stop, unless it would be unsafe to do so.
d) All other lights will be showing red.

2   A theory test pass certificate is valid for:

a) 6 months.
b) 12 months.
c) 18 months.
d) 24 months.

3   Signs giving directions are usually:

a) Rectangular.
b) Triangular.
c) Circular.
d) Hexagonal.

4   A long white with short gaps down the centre of the road is an indication of:

a) A deviation.
b) An entrance to property.
c) A hazard.
d) An urban clearway.

5   *The Highway Code* says that you should never reverse:

a) From a major road into a minor road.
b) On one-way streets.
c) From a minor road onto a major road.
d) Into narrow driveways.

6   Reflective studs along the left edge of the road are:

a) Blue.
b) White.
c) Amber.
d) Red.

7   Pupils should apply for the theory test:

a) Within three months of receiving their provisional licence.
b) When they have studied and the ADI advises them to do so.
c) Only after they have had some practical lessons.
d) Only after passing the hazard perception test.

8 Unless exempt, passengers travelling in cars must wear seat belts in:

a) The front seats only.
b) Any seat of the car.
c) The rear seats only.
d) Towns and on motorways only.

9 You must report to the licensing authority any medical condition that:

a) Warrants a visit to the doctor.
b) Is likely to last more than one month.
c) Is likely to last more than three months.
d) Requires you to take medication.

10 Car passengers under three years of age are the responsibility of:

a) Their parents.
b) The adult sitting next to them.
c) No one in particular.
d) The driver.

11 The speed limits for learner drivers are:

a) The same as for full licence holders.
b) 10 mph less than for full licence holders.
c) 10 per cent less than for full licence holders.
d) Maximum 50 mph.

12 You should control the speed of your car when driving downhill by:

a) Using the highest gear possible.
b) Slowing down and then changing to a lower gear.
c) Coasting while using the footbrake.
d) Braking firmly all the way down the hill.

13 The maximum legal alcohol/breath limit is:

a) 40 microgrammes/100 ml.
b) 45 microgrammes/100 ml.
c) 30 microgrammes/100 ml.
d) 35 microgrammes/100 ml.

14 To ensure uniformity of tests, examiners are:

a) Allowed to apply their own standards to individual tests.
b) Never transferred from one test centre to another.
c) Closely supervised by a senior examiner.
d) Influenced by each ADI's standards.

15 A full driving licence is valid until the driver's:

a) 60th birthday.
b) 65th birthday.
c) 70th birthday.
d) 75th birthday.

16 If you are involved in an accident and do not have your insurance certificate with you, it must be produced at a police station within:

a) 24 hours.
b) 48 hours.
c) five days.
d) seven days.

17 Children under 14 should wear seat belts:

a) If travelling in the front or rear of the car.
b) When they are the only passenger in the car.
c) If they decide for themselves to do so.
d) Only if there is no child harness available.

18 In built-up areas, a 30 mph speed limit applies unless there are:

a) Signs indicating otherwise.
b) Houses on one side of the road.
c) Signs stating 'urban clearway'.
d) No pavements.

19 A provisional licence holder is allowed to drive a vehicle of up to:

a) 1.5 tonnes.
b) 3.5 tonnes.
c) 7.5 tonnes
d) 2.0 tonnes.

20 Using the gears to slow down should:

a) Result in better fuel economy.
b) Be normal practice for learners.
c) Not be normal practice.
d) Save wear and tear on the gearbox.

21 Groups of people marching on the road should:

a) Keep to the right.
b) Keep to the left.
c) Have a red flag showing at the back of the group.
d) Have a white flag showing at the front of the group.

22 Approaching a green traffic light, you should:

a) Speed up in case the light changes.
b) Give an arm signal for slowing down.
c) Expect traffic in other directions to stop.
d) Be ready to stop if the lights change.

23 When walking with children, you should:

a) Cross the road only at pedestrian crossings.
b) Walk between the child and the road.
c) Make sure the child is wearing reflective clothing.
d) Cross the road with the child in front.

24   Unless you are receiving higher-rate Disability Living Allowance, the minimum legal age for driving a car is:

  a) 17.
  b) 16.
  c) 18.
  d) 21.

25   As a general rule, driving test routes are designed to incorporate:

  a) A wide variety of road and traffic situations.
  b) Level crossings or motorways.
  c) Very steep gradients.
  d) As many non-standard situations as possible.

26   The ADI Regulations are part of:

  a) The Road Traffic Act.
  b) Your Road to Becoming an Approved Driving Instructor.
  c) *The Official Guide to Learning to Drive.*
  d) *The Driving Instructor's Handbook.*

27   When turning right, at a junction where an oncoming vehicle is also turning right, the DSA book, *Driving – the essential skills*, advises:

  a) Turning nearside to nearside.
  b) Turning offside to offside where possible.
  c) Holding back until the road is clear.
  d) Waiting behind the give-way line.

28   According to *The Highway Code*, you should not park on:

  a) The right-hand side of the road.
  b) Any broken yellow line at night.
  c) Any road where there are no street lights.
  d) A road marked with double white lines.

29   *The Highway Code* says that, at night, you should use:

  a) Sidelights in built-up areas.
  b) Dipped headlights in built-up areas.
  c) Sidelights on all roads.
  d) Sidelights and fog lights.

30   Serious faults committed by the pupil in the first few minutes of a driving test:

  a) Will be ignored by the examiner.
  b) Never result in failure.
  c) Will not be recorded.
  d) May result in failure.

31 One of the basic teaching principles is:

a) Demonstration–practice–explanation.
b) Practice–explanation–demonstration.
c) Explanation–demonstration–practice.
d) Explanation–practice–demonstration.

32 When attending for a theory test, candidates must produce:

a) A current valid provisional driving licence.
b) A copy of *The Official Guide to Learning to Drive*.
c) Acknowledgement of their application.
d) Their instructor's ADI certificate.

33 The instruction for turning left should be:

a) Turn next left, please.
b) Next left turn, please.
c) Take the next opening on the left, please.
d) Take the next road on the left, please.

34 For an instructor to accompany a pupil on test, the:

a) Candidate must ask the examiner.
b) Instructor must ask the examiner.
c) Request must be made on the original application.
d) Instructor must sign not to take part.

35 *The Highway Code* says that the minimum tread on tyres should be:

a) 1.0 mm.
b) 1.6 mm.
c) 2.0 mm
d) 2.6 mm.

36 A white stick with a red band is used by someone who is:

a) Blind and mute.
b) Partially sighted.
c) Deaf and blind.
d) Registered as blind

37 A pupil on test who commits only one serious fault will:

a) Pass the test.
b) Fail the test.
c) Be judged at the examiner's discretion.
d) Be taken back to the test centre.

38 To cancel a driving test without losing the fee requires:

a) Three complete working days' notice.
b) Three days' notice including weekend days.
c) Three days' notice including Bank Holidays.
d) Three days' notice including the day of the test.

39   When first introducing a novice to the use of mirrors emphasis should be placed on:

a) Correct adjustment.
b) Effective use of all mirrors.
c) Full, all-round observations.
d) Checking the nearside blind areas.

40   For a first attempt at reversing most emphasis should be on:

a) Taking effective observations.
b) Maintaining control of the car.
c) Finishing in a perfect position.
d) Using the handbrake at each pause.

41   According to the DSA book, *Driving – the essential skills*, it is:

a) Essential that an ADI is a 'perfect driver'.
b) Doubtful that the 'perfect driver' exists.
c) Quite common to achieve driving perfection.
d) Not worth aiming for perfection in your driving.

42   Anyone supervising a learner driver must:

a) Be at least 25 and have held a full driving licence for at least three years.
b) Have passed an advanced driving test.
c) Have their name on the ADI register or hold a trainee licence.
d) Be at least 21 and have held a full driving licence for that type of vehicle for at least three years.

43   If an examiner has to take action, this will be recorded on the driving test report as a:

a) Possible failure.
b) Driving fault.
c) Serious fault.
d) Dangerous fault.

44   Who, of the following, may accompany a learner on a driving test:

a) Anyone the candidate wishes.
b) Only an ADI.
c) Only a parent or guardian.
d) No one other than DSA personnel.

45   The purpose of the examiner's driving report, which is given to all successful test candidates, is to:

a) Help overcome any minor weaknesses in the candidate's driving.
b) Show how close to perfect the candidate was.
c) Make sure the successful candidate does not become over confident.
d) Highlight the errors in the ADI's teaching.

46   So that learners get the most benefit from each lesson, instructors should organize their teaching plan:

   a) At the beginning of each session.
   b) In short, attainable stages.
   c) In large stages, so that fewer lessons will be needed.
   d) Extensively to cover all aspects.

47   Setting very difficult objectives for a learner driver may:

   a) Help pupils learn more quickly.
   b) Slow down the pupil's learning.
   c) Cause pupils to lose concentration.
   d) Result in more being remembered.

48   At the end of each lesson the instructor should:

   a) Point out all the faults committed during the lesson.
   b) Emphasize each individual fault.
   c) Take the payment for the next lesson.
   d) Recap on what has been learnt.

49   When passing stationary buses you should:

   a) Drive past quickly to minimize the danger.
   b) Pass slowly, looking for people getting off.
   c) Flash your headlights to warn the driver.
   d) Sound the horn to warn any pedestrians.

50   When students reach a 'plateau' in their learning you should:

   a) Go on to a new topic.
   b) Carry on with the lesson you had planned.
   c) Return to a previous topic for reinforcement purposes.
   d) Introduce a more difficult topic.

51   Extreme emotions such as fear or anger:

   a) Can be relieved by going for a drive.
   b) Can enhance concentration when driving.
   c) Should help you to pay attention to hazards.
   d) Can reduce your concentration levels.

52   The exhaust system:

   a) Gets rid of burnt gases.
   b) Only works when the engine is hot.
   c) Takes hot air from the carburettor.
   d) Helps to slow the car.

53   If your car breaks down on a level crossing and the bells start ringing, you should firstly:

   a) Push the vehicle over the crossing.
   b) Try to find out the cause of the problem.
   c) Stand well clear.
   d) Wave a warning signal.

54   An ADI who is disqualified from driving for 12 months would be barred from giving driving instruction for a total of:

   a) One year.
   b) Two years.
   c) Five years.
   d) Six years.

55   You can only be issued with a trainee licence if you:

   a) Are preparing for the ADI exams.
   b) Have passed Parts 1 and 2 and are sponsored by an ADI.
   c) Have passed Part 1 of the ADI exam.
   d) Are taking training with an authorized training organization.

56   If you are first to arrive at the scene of an accident and a casualty stops breathing, you should:

   a) Tilt their head forward.
   b) First check that their airway is clear.
   c) Not move their head.
   d) Put a pillow under their head.

57   If you are involved in an accident which involves someone else, you should first of all:

   a) Drive to the nearest police station.
   b) Check your car for damage before driving on.
   c) Phone home to let someone know.
   d) Stop immediately and exchange details.

58   If a police officer asks you to produce your documents, they must be taken to:

   a) A police station nominated by the officer.
   b) A police station of your choice.
   c) Police headquarters.
   d) The nearest police station.

59   The three main factors involved in a skid are:

   a) Driver, vehicle, weather.
   b) Vehicle, road, weather.
   c) Driver, number of passengers, road.
   d) Driver, vehicle, road.

60 You should 'make progress' by:

a) Always driving up to the speed limit.
b) Changing up to the highest gear as soon as possible.
c) Always keeping up with other drivers.
d) Driving at speeds to suit the conditions.

61 In fog, when waiting to turn right into a side road, you should:

a) Keep your right foot on the brake pedal.
b) Use the hazard warning flashers.
c) Keep well over to the left side of the road.
d) Give an arm signal as an extra warning.

62 Approaching a junction in an unfamiliar area, you should:

a) Select the centre lane.
b) Be guided by the signs and road markings.
c) Always position well to the left to be on the safe side.
d) Always stop and ask the way.

63 When driving downhill gravity makes:

a) The brakes more effective.
b) No difference to the braking.
c) The brakes less effective.
d) It necessary to use the ABS.

64 Parking at the kerb on the left facing uphill, you should:

a) Put a brick behind each wheel.
b) Keep the wheels straight.
c) Turn the steering wheel to the left.
d) Turn the steering wheel to the right.

65 When driving on multi-lane roads you should keep:

a) Close to the lane marking on your left.
b) Close to the lane marking on your right.
c) In the centre of your lane.
d) As far to the left as you can.

66 Before crossing a one way street, pedestrians should look:

a) To the left.
b) To the right.
c) Both ways.
d) All around.

67 The PSL routine is used:

a) Instead of the MSM routine.
b) As part of the MSM routine.
c) Before the MSM routine.
d) Only as part of an overtaking manoeuvre.

68 You may wait in a box junction when:

  a) The exit is clear and you intend to turn right.
  b) You are following the road ahead.
  c) You are turning left, but your exit is blocked.
  d) Your filter light is showing green.

69 *The Highway Code* states that you must not reverse for more than:

  a) The distance you can see to be clear.
  b) 10 metres.
  c) 14 metres.
  d) The distance that is necessary.

70 At zebra crossings you must not pass:

  a) The moving vehicle nearest the crossing.
  b) Any moving vehicle within the zig zags.
  c) Any vehicle when you are approaching the crossing.
  d) Any cyclist.

71 Anti-lock braking systems

  a) Are only built into cars with automatic transmission.
  b) Prevent the car from skidding.
  c) Only work when braking gently.
  d) Are designed to prevent the wheels locking during heavy braking.

72 People with disabilities are:

  a) Permitted to drive adapted cars only.
  b) Restricted to driving cars with automatic transmission.
  c) Not allowed to drive on motorways.
  d) Permitted to drive any type of car, depending on their disability.

73 Flashing headlights should be used:

  a) As a warning of your presence.
  b) When giving way to other drivers.
  c) When you are dazzled by oncoming headlights.
  d) When you are greeting another driver.

74 When turning from a main road into a side road, give way to:

  a) All pedestrians who are waiting.
  b) Traffic coming from your left.
  c) All the traffic in the road you are turning into.
  d) Pedestrians who are crossing the road.

75 Approaching a roundabout, you should:

  a) Stop at the give-way line.
  b) Keep moving if the way is clear.
  c) Give way to all traffic.
  d) Always change down to second gear.

76. For pedestrians, the flashing green man at pelican crossings means:

 a) Cross the road with care.
 b) Do not start to cross.
 c) Cross the road quickly.
 d) Drivers have priority over pedestrians.

77 When crossing a dual carriageway you should:

 a) Wait in the side road until you can cross both carriageways.
 b) Cross one half, then wait in the central reservation until the second half is clear.
 c) Take into account the width of the central reservation before deciding on how to cross.
 d) Turn left onto the dual carriageway, then turn round.

78 The main reason for a skid to occur is the:

 a) Condition of the car.
 b) Condition of the road surface.
 c) Driver not responding to the conditions.
 d) Lack of grit or sand on the road.

79 When reversing in a van, it is usually better to:

 a) Reverse into an opening on the right.
 b) Reverse into an opening on the left.
 c) Use the interior mirrors to get a better view.
 d) Get your passenger to guide you.

80 When waiting to turn right at a box junction where there is oncoming traffic you should wait:

 a) In the yellow box.
 b) At the stop line.
 c) In the box only if your exit is blocked.
 d) Until the light has changed to red.

81 A green filter arrow means.

 a) Only proceed when the main green light is showing.
 b) Proceed if it's safe to do so, regardless of the other light.
 c) All the other lights will be showing red.
 d) It is now safe for you to proceed.

82 Learner drivers should use mirrors to:

 a) Decide if their actions will be safe.
 b) Show examiners that they are using them.
 c) Check if the mirrors are adjusted correctly.
 d) Check all the blind areas around the car.

83 High-intensity rear fog lights should be used:

a) If visibility falls below 100 metres.
b) Whenever it is misty or raining.
c) When driving on unlit roads.
d) When a following driver is too close.

84 If a candidate attends for the practical test in a car that appears to be un-roadworthy:

a) Another appointment will be given at no extra cost.
b) The candidate will be advised to have the car checked over after the test.
c) The facts will be reported to DVLA.
d) The test may be cancelled, with no refund.

85 When following other traffic on a dry road, you should leave a time gap of at least:

a) five seconds.
b) four seconds.
c) three seconds.
d) two seconds.

86 Driving test candidates who make a lot of driving faults, but which are not considered serious or dangerous:

a) May fail the test.
b) Are not likely to fail unless a serious or dangerous is made.
c) Are likely to make the examiner nervous.
d) Will be obliged to take a further theory test.

87 *The Highway Code* recommends the use of an arm signal when:

a) Turning right or left into a driveway.
b) Stopping at a pedestrian crossing.
c) Stopping on the right-hand side of the road.
d) When taking your driving test.

88 Your following distance on wet roads should be:

a) Doubled.
b) Trebled.
c) Quadrupled.
d) Twice your distance.

89 According to the DSA book, *Driving – the essential skills*, the only safe separation distance is:

a) Your thinking distance.
b) Your overall stopping distance.
c) Your normal following distance.
d) At least two cars' lengths behind others.

90. Pedestrians should show their intention to cross at a zebra crossing by:
    a) Waiting by the beacon.
    b) Raising a hand to approaching drivers.
    c) Stepping onto the give-way line.
    d) Putting one foot on the crossing.

91 At 70 mph the braking distance is:
    a) 21m (70ft).
    b) 38m (125ft).
    c) 75m (245ft).
    d) 96m (315ft).

92 Fuel economy can be maximized by:
    a) Using all the gears progressively when slowing down.
    b) Using engine braking as much as possible.
    c) Using the lowest gears possible.
    d) Using the highest gear possible.

93 When applying for a test for a pupil who has a slight disability, you should:
    a) Not mention it on the application form.
    b) Give as much information as possible.
    c) Inform the DSA at Nottingham.
    d) Tell the examiner on the day of the test.

94 When dealing with bends the speed of the car should be lowest when you are:
    a) Entering the bend.
    b) Halfway round the bend.
    c) Leaving the bend.
    d) Approaching the bend.

95 Flashing headlights mean the:
    a) Same as sounding the horn.
    b) Oncoming driver is giving way.
    c) Oncoming driver is proceeding.
    d) Road is clear for oncoming vehicles.

96 If you break down on a level crossing you must first of all:
    a) Push the vehicle clear of the crossing.
    b) Stand well clear.
    c) Get your passengers out.
    d) Use your mobile phone to get help.

97 Before emerging at a junction, your pupil should:

a) Keep looking to the right for traffic.
b) Look right, left, then right again.
c) Look left–right, left–right.
d) Look effectively in all directions.

98 The clutch separates the:

a) Fuel and air mixture.
b) Footbrake and handbrake.
c) Drive between engine and wheels.
d) Transmission from the steering

99 *The Highway Code* advises signalling:

a) As often as possible.
b) To warn or inform others.
c) For moving off and stopping.
d) Only when you can't see into a side road.

100 If the road ahead is flooded, you should:

a) Stop and check the depth of the water.
b) Drive through as quickly as possible.
c) Drive over the verge to avoid the deeper water.
d) Check the brakes before driving through.

APPENDIX I
Useful addresses

Driving Standards Agency (DSA)
The Axis Building
112 Upper Parliament Street
Nottingham
NG1 6LP
Tel: 0300 200 1122
www.dft.gov.uk/dsa

Driving and Vehicle Licensing Agency (DVLA)
Longview Road
Swansea
SA6 7JL
Tel: 01792 782 341
www.dvla.gov.uk
e-mail: vehicles.dvla@gtnet.gov.uk

Driver and Vehicle Agency (DVA)
66 Balmoral Road
Belfast
BT12 6QL
028 9054 7933
www.dvtani.gov.uk

Instructor organizations

Approved Driving Instructors National Joint Council (ADINJC)
47 Sweetmans Road
Shaftesbury
Dorset
SP7 8EH
Tel: 01747 855091;
e-mail: liaisonofficer@ adinjc.org.uk
www.adinjc.org.uk

Driving Instructors Association (DIA)
Safety House
Beddington Farm Road
Croydon
Surrey
CR0 4XZ
Tel: 020 8665 5151 or 0845 345 5151
e-mail: DIA@driving.org;
www.driving.org

Driving Instructors Democratic Union (A branch of UNITE)
Chairman, DIDU
Transport House
55 Call Lane
Leeds
LS1 7BW
Tel: 05602 609125
e-mail: info@didu.org.uk
www.didu.org.uk

Driving Instructors Scottish Council (DISC)
4 Burnside Road
Uphall Broxburn
West Lothian
EH52 5DE
Tel: 01506 855455
e-mail: aeneas.disc@tiscali.co.uk;
www.d-i-s-c.org.uk

Motor Schools Association GB Ltd (MSA)
101 Wellington Road North
Stockport
Cheshire
SK4 2LP
Tel: 0161 429 9669
e-mail: mail@msagb.co.uk
www.msagb.co.uk

SmartDriving
Ballinultha
Boyle
County Roscommon
Ireland
www.smartdriving co.uk

Training aids and services

Desk Top Driving Ltd
Unit 6, Gaugemaster Way
Ford
Arundel
West Sussex
BN18 0RX
Tel: 01903 882299
www.desktopdriving.co.uk

Driving School Aids
Low Lane
Horsforth
West Yorks
LS18 4DD
Tel: 0113 258 0688

Driving School Supplies
2–4 Tame Road
Witton
Birmingham
B6 7DS
Tel: 0121 328 6226
www.d-ss.co.uk

He-Man Dual Controls Ltd
Cable Street
Southampton
SO14 5AR
Tel: 023 8022 6952
www.he-mandualcontrols.co.uk

Porter Dual Controls
Impact Business Park
Greenford
Middlesex
UB6 7JD
Tel: 020 8601 3566

RCM Marketing Ltd
20 Newtown Business Park
Albion Close
Poole
Dorset
BH12 3LL
Tel: 01202 737999
www.rcmmarketing.co.uk

The Stationery Office (TSO)
St Crispins
Duke Street
Norwich
NR3 1PD
Tel: 01603 622211
www.tso.co.uk

Wholesale Book Supplies
18 High Street
Bala
Gwynedd
LL23 7AG
Tel: 0800 195 2208
www.wholesalebooks.co.uk

Motoring organizations

Automobile Association
Member Administration Contact Centre
Lambert House
Stockport Road
Cheadle
SK8 2DY
Tel: 0870 600 0371
Disability helpline: 0800 26 20 50
www.theaa.com

Royal Automobile Club
Customer Services
Great Park Road
Bradley Stoke
Bristol
BS32 4QN
Tel: 08705 722 722
www.rac.co.uk

APPENDIX II
Further reading; reference books

Your Road to Becoming an Approved Driving Instructor
(ADI 14), Driving Standards Agency (DSA)
The starter pack for potential driving instructors. Available as a free download from www.direct.gov.uk or www.desktopdriving.co.uk.

The Official DSA Guide to Driving – The essential skills
DSA/The Stationery Office
Comprehensive guidance on driving skills for all drivers and instructors

The Official Guide to Learning to Drive
DSA/The Stationery Office
Explains the standards required to pass the driving test. Includes a section on independent driving.

Know Your Traffic Signs
DSA/The Stationery Office
Illustrates and describes most of the UK road and traffic signs you will encounter.

The Official Highway Code
DSA/The Stationery Office
Essential reading for all road users.

The Driving Instructor's Handbook (17th edn) – by John Miller and Margaret Stacey
Published by Kogan Page
Recognized as the industry standard and the authoritive guide for ADIs and PDIs.
Listed by the DSA as essential reading material for the ADI exams.

Practical Teaching Skills for Driving Instructors (8th edn) – John Miller
and Margaret Stacey
Published by Kogan Page
How to develop and improve your coaching and teaching skills. Deals with
communication, motivation and how people learn.
Listed by the DSA as essential reading for the ADI exams.

Instructional Techniques and Practice – Les Walklin
Published by Stanley Thornes
Covers the theory and practice of teaching, learning and assessing.
Listed by the DSA as essential reading for the ADI exams.

APPENDIX III
Answers for example DSA questions (Chapter 2)

1.1 A pelican crossing that crosses the road in a straight line and has a central island must be treated as:

– one complete crossing.

1.2 You wish to overtake a long, slow-moving vehicle on a busy road. You should:

– keep well back until you can see that it is clear.

1.3 You have been involved in an argument before starting your journey. This has made you feel angry. You should:

– calm down before you start to drive.

1.4 You think the driver of the vehicle in front has forgotten to cancel the right indicator. You should:

– stay behind and not overtake.

1.5 A driver pulls out of a side road in front of you. You have to brake hard. You should:

– ignore the error and stay calm.

1.6 You are in a line of traffic. The driver behind you is following very closely. What action should you take?

– Slow down, gradually increasing the gap between you and the vehicle in front.

1.7 What action would you take when elderly people are crossing the road?

– Be patient and allow them to cross in their own time.

1.8 There is a slow-moving vehicle ahead of you. You are unsure what the driver is going to do. You should:

– stay behind.

1.9 You are waiting to emerge left from a minor road. A large vehicle is approaching from the right. You have time to turn but should wait because the large vehicle:

– can easily hide an overtaking vehicle.

1.10 Some two way roads are divided into three lanes. These are particularly dangerous because traffic:

– in both directions can use the middle lane to overtake.

2.1 What colour are the reflective studs between a motorway and its slip road?

– Green.

2.2 Yellow lines across the road on the approach to roundabouts are to:

– make you aware of your speed.

2.3 Why should you NOT coast downhill?

– You have less control of your vehicle.

2.4 Your car starts to skid and the rear wheels are sliding to the left. You should:

– steer to the left.

2.5 When reversing a car in a straight line you:

– may steer with one hand if this helps.

2.6 If the power fails on a power assisted steering system this will result in:

– more effort needed to turn the steering wheel.

2.7 At a toucan crossing:

– there is no flashing amber light.

2.8 You see a pedestrian with a white stick and red band. This means that the person is:

– deaf and blind.

2.9 Catalytic converters are fitted to make the:

– exhaust fumes cleaner.

3.1 During the driving test a candidate makes a smooth direct gear change from fourth to second gear. The examiner observing this action would assess this as being:

– satisfactory.

3.2 At the start of a driving test a candidate finds that their inertia reel seat belt has temporarily locked and they cannot put it on. They should:

– put it on as soon as the belt is released.

3.3 A person who is blind in one eye is:

– permitted to drive a motor car.

3.4 You leave your vehicle overnight on a road with a 40 mph speed limit. You should park:

– with parking lights on.

3.5 You are not allowed to travel in the right hand lane of a three-lane motorway, if you are driving a:

– vehicle towing a trailer.

3.6 It is a driver's responsibility to ensure that the front seat passenger wears a seat belt if the passenger is under:

– 14 years old.

3.7 Learner drivers in a car must be supervised by someone who is:

– 21 (or over) and who has held a full licence for that category of vehicle for at least 3 years.

4.1 Which of these vehicles might you find using a flashing amber light on a dual carriageway?

– A disabled person's vehicle.

4.2 Why are hatch markings painted in the centre of the road?

– To separate traffic flowing in opposite directions.

4.3 To help a pupil attain a good standard of driving the amount of verbal instruction should be:

– reduced as their competence increases.

4.4 As an aid to progressive learning a pupil's progress on a course should be measured:

– as an ongoing assessment.

4.5 The 'learning plateau' sometimes occurs during training. This refers to:

– a temporary halt in the learning process.

4.6 Learning by rote is an appropriate teaching method for:

– memorising facts and figures.

4.7 Having decided upon a lesson plan for a particular pupil, an instructor should:

– alter the lesson plan if necessary.

4.8 An instructor observes a driving fault committed by the pupil. This should be:

– used as a teaching point.

APPENDIX IV
Mock test answers

1 At traffic lights, amber means:

c) Stop, unless it would be unsafe to do so.

2 A theory test pass certificate is valid for:

d) 24 months.

3 Signs giving directions are usually:

a) Rectangular.

4 A long white with short gaps down the centre of the road is an indication of:

c) A hazard.

5 *The Highway Code* says that you should never reverse:

c) From a minor road onto a major road.

6 Reflective studs along the left edge of the road are:

d) Red.

7 Pupils should apply for the Theory Test:

b) When they have studied and the ADI advises them to do so.

8 Unless exempt, passengers travelling in cars must wear seat belts in:

b) Any seat of the car.

9 You must report to the licensing authority any medical condition that:

c) Is likely to last more than three months.

10 Car passengers under three years of age are the responsibility of:

d) The driver.

11 The speed limits for learner drivers are:

a) The same as for full licence holders.

12 You should control the speed of your car when driving downhill by:

b) Slowing down and then changing to a lower gear.

13 The maximum legal alcohol/breath limit is:

   d) 35 microgrammes / 100 ml.

14 To ensure uniformity of tests, examiners are:

   c) Closely supervised by a senior examiner.

15 A full driving licence is valid until the driver's:

   c) 70th birthday.

16 If you are involved in an accident and do not have your insurance certificate with you, it must be produced at a police station within:

   d) Seven days.

17 Children under 14 should wear seat belts.

   a) If travelling in the front or rear of the car.

18 In built-up areas, a 30 mph speed limit applies unless there are:

   a) Signs indicating otherwise.

19 A provisional licence holder is allowed to drive a vehicle of up to:

   b) 3.5 tonnes.

20 Using the gears to slow down should:

   c) Not be normal practice.

21 Groups of people marching on the road should:

   b) Keep to the left.

22 Approaching a green traffic light, you should:

   d) Be ready to stop if the lights change.

23 When walking with children, you should:

   b) Walk between the child and the road.

24 Unless you are receiving higher-rate Disability Living Allowance, the minimum legal age for driving a car is:

   a) 17.

25 As a general rule, driving test routes are designed to incorporate:

   a) A wide variety of road and traffic situations.

26 The ADI regulations are part of:

   a) The Road Traffic Act.

27 When turning right, at a junction where an oncoming vehicle is also turning right, the DSA book, *Driving – the essential skills*, advises:

   b) Turning offside to offside where possible.

28 According to *The Highway Code*, you should not park on:
    d) A road marked with double white lines.

29 *The Highway Code* says that, at night, you should use:
    b) Dipped headlights in built-up areas.

30 Serious faults committed by the pupil in the first few minutes of a driving test:
    d) May result in failure.

31 One of the basic teaching principles is:
    c) Explanation–demonstration–practice.

32 When attending for a theory test, candidates must produce:
    a) A current valid provisional driving licence.

33 The instruction for turning left should be:
    d) Take the next road on the left, please.

34. For an instructor to accompany a pupil on test, the:
    a) Candidate must ask the examiner.

35 *The Highway Code* says that the minimum tread on tyres should be:
    b) 1.6 mm.

36 A white stick with a red band is used by someone who is:
    c) Deaf and blind.

37 A pupil on test who commits only one serious fault will:
    b) Fail the test.

38 To cancel a driving test without losing the fee requires:
    a) Three complete working days' notice.

39 When first introducing a novice to the use of mirrors emphasis should be placed on:
    a) Correct adjustment.

40 For a first attempt at reversing most emphasis should be on:
    b) Maintaining control of the car.

41 According to the DSA book, *Driving – the essential skills*, it is:
    b) Doubtful that the 'perfect driver' exists.

42 Anyone supervising a learner driver must:
    d) Be at least 21 and have held a full driving licence for that type of vehicle for at least three years.

43 If an examiner has to take action, this will be recorded on the driving test report as a:

d) Dangerous fault.

44 Who, of the following, may accompany a learner on a driving test?

a) Anyone the candidate wishes.

45 The purpose of the examiner's driving report, which is given to all successful test candidates, is to:

a) Help overcome any minor weaknesses in the candidate's driving.

46 So that learners get the most benefit from each lesson, instructors should organize their teaching plan:

b) In short, attainable stages.

47 Setting very difficult objectives for a learner driver may:

b) Slow down the pupil's learning.

48 At the end of each lesson the instructor should:

d) Recap on what has been learnt.

49 When passing stationary buses you should:

b) Pass slowly, looking for people getting off.

50 When students reach a 'plateau' in their learning you should:

c) Return to a previous topic for reinforcement purposes.

51 Extreme emotions such as fear or anger:

d) Can reduce your concentration levels.

52 The exhaust system:

a) Gets rid of burnt gases.

53 If your car breaks down on a level crossing and the bells start ringing, you should firstly:

c) Stand well clear.

54 An ADI who is disqualified from driving for 12 months would be barred from giving driving instruction for a total of:

c) Five years.

55 You can only be issued with a trainee licence if you:

b) Have passed Parts 1 and 2 and are sponsored by an ADI.

56 If you are first to arrive at the scene of an accident and a casualty stops breathing, you should:

b) First check that their airway is clear.

57   If you are involved in an accident which involves someone else, you should first of all:

d) Stop immediately and exchange details.

58   If a police officer asks you to produce your documents, they must be taken to:

b) A police station of your choice.

59   The three main factors involved in a skid are:

d) Driver, vehicle, road.

60   You should 'make progress' by:

d) Driving at speeds to suit the conditions.

61   In fog, when waiting to turn right into a side road, you should:

a) Keep your right foot on the brake pedal.

62   Approaching a junction in an unfamiliar area, you should:

b) Be guided by the signs and road markings.

63   When driving downhill gravity makes:

c) The brakes less effective.

64   Parking at the kerb on the left facing uphill, you should:

d) Turn the steering wheel to the right.

65   When driving on multi-lane roads you should keep:

c) In the centre of your lane.

66   Before crossing a one way street, pedestrians should look:

c) Both ways.

67   The PSL routine is used:

b) as part of the MSM routine.

68   You may wait in a box junction when:

a) The exit is clear and you intend to turn right.

69   *The Highway Code* states that you must not reverse for more than:

d) The distance that is necessary.

70   At zebra crossings you must not pass:

a) The moving vehicle nearest the crossing.

71   Anti-lock braking systems

d) Are designed to prevent the wheels locking during heavy braking.

72   People with disabilities are:

d) Permitted to drive any type of car, depending on their disability.

73 Flashing headlights should be used:

a) As a warning of your presence.

74 When turning from a main road into a side road, give way to:

d) Pedestrians who are crossing the road.

75 Approaching a roundabout, you should:

b) Keep moving if the way is clear.

76 For pedestrians, the flashing green man at pelican crossings means:

b) Do not start to cross.

77 When crossing a dual carriageway you should:

c) Take into account the width of the central reservation before deciding on how to cross.

78 The main reason for a skid to occur is the:

c) Driver not responding to the conditions.

79 When reversing in a van, it is usually better to:

a) Reverse into an opening on the right.

80 When waiting to turn right at a box junction where there is oncoming traffic you should wait:

a) In the yellow box.

81 A green filter arrow means:

b) Proceed if it's safe to do so, regardless of the other light.

82 Learner drivers should use mirrors to:

a) Decide if their actions will be safe.

83 High-intensity rear fog lights should be used:

a) If visibility falls below 100 metres.

84 If a candidate attends for the practical test in a car that appears to be un-roadworthy:

d) The test may be cancelled, with no refund.

85 When following other traffic on a dry road, you should leave a time gap of at least:

d) 2 seconds.

86 Driving test candidates who make a lot of driving faults, but which are not considered serious or dangerous:

a) May fail the test.

87 *The Highway Code* recommends the use of an arm signal when:

b) Stopping at a pedestrian crossing.

88 Your following distance on wet roads should be:

a) Doubled.

89 According to the DSA book, *Driving – the essential skills*, the only safe separation distance is:

b) Your overall stopping distance.

90 Pedestrians should show their intention to cross at a zebra crossing by:

d) Putting one foot on the crossing.

91 At 70mph the braking distance is:

c) 75m (245ft).

92 Fuel economy can be maximized by:

d) Using the highest gear possible.

93 When applying for a test for a pupil who has a slight disability, you should:

b) Give as much information as possible.

94 When dealing with bends the speed of the car should be lowest when you are:

a) Entering the bend.

95 Flashing headlights mean the:

a) Same as sounding the horn.

96 If you break down on a level crossing you must first of all:

c) Get your passengers out.

97 Before emerging at a junction, your pupil should:

d) Look effectively in all directions.

98 The clutch separates the:

c) Drive between engine and wheels.

99 *The Highway Code* advises signalling:

b) To warn or inform others.

100 If the road ahead is flooded, you should:

a) Stop and check the depth of the water.

APPENDIX V
Theory test centres

England

Aldershot, Barnstable, Barrow, Basildon, Basingstoke, Bath, Berwick-upon-Tweed, Birkenhead, Birmingham, Blackpool, Bolton, Boston, Bournemouth, Bradford, Brighton, Bristol, Bury St Edmunds, Cambridge, Canterbury, Carlisle, Chelmsford, Cheltenham, Chester, Chesterfield, Colchester, Coventry, Crawley, Derby, Doncaster, Dudley, Durham, Eastbourne, Exeter, Fareham, Gillingham, Gloucester, Grantham, Grimsby, Guildford, Harlow, Harrogate, Hastings, Hereford, Huddersfield, Hull, Ipswich, Isle of Wight, Isles of Scilly, Kings Lynn, Leeds, Leicester, Lincoln, Liverpool, London (Croydon, Ilford, Kingston, Southgate, Southwark, Staines, Uxbridge), Lowestoft, Luton, Manchester, Mansfield, Middlesbrough, Milton Keynes, Morpeth, Newcastle, Northampton, Norwich, Nottingham, Oldham, Oxford, Penzance, Peterborough, Plymouth, Portsmouth, Preston, Reading, Redditch, Runcorn, Salford, Salisbury, Scarborough, Scunthorpe, Sheffield, Shrewsbury, Sidcup, Slough, Solihull, Southampton, Southend-on-Sea, Southport, St Helens, Stevenage, Stockport, Stoke on Trent, Stratford-upon-Avon, Sunderland, Sutton Coldfield, Swindon, Taunton, Torquay, Truro, Watford, Weymouth, Wigan, Wolverhampton, Worcester, Workington, Worthing, Yeovil, York

Scotland

Aberdeen, Ayr, Dumfries, Dundee, Dunfermline, Edinburgh, Elgin, Fort William, Gairloch, Galashiels, Glasgow (Clydebank), Greenock, Helmsdale, Huntly, Inverness, Isle of Arran, Isle of Benbecula, Isle of Islay (Bowmore), Isle of Mull (Salen), Isle of Tiree, Kirkwall, Kyle of Lochalsh, Lerwick, Motherwell, Oban, Pitlochry, Portree, Stirling, Stornoway, Stranraer, Tarbet, Tongue, Ullapool, Wick

Wales

Aberystwyth, Bangor, Builth Wells, Cardiff, Haverfordwest, Merthyr Tydfil, Newport, Rhyll, Swansea

Northern Ireland

Ballymena, Belfast, Londonderry, Newry, Omagh, Portadown

INDEX

INDEX OF ADVERTISERS